Sawyer

William Roy 1726–1790

Published for THE BRITISH LIBRARY by British Museum Publications Ltd

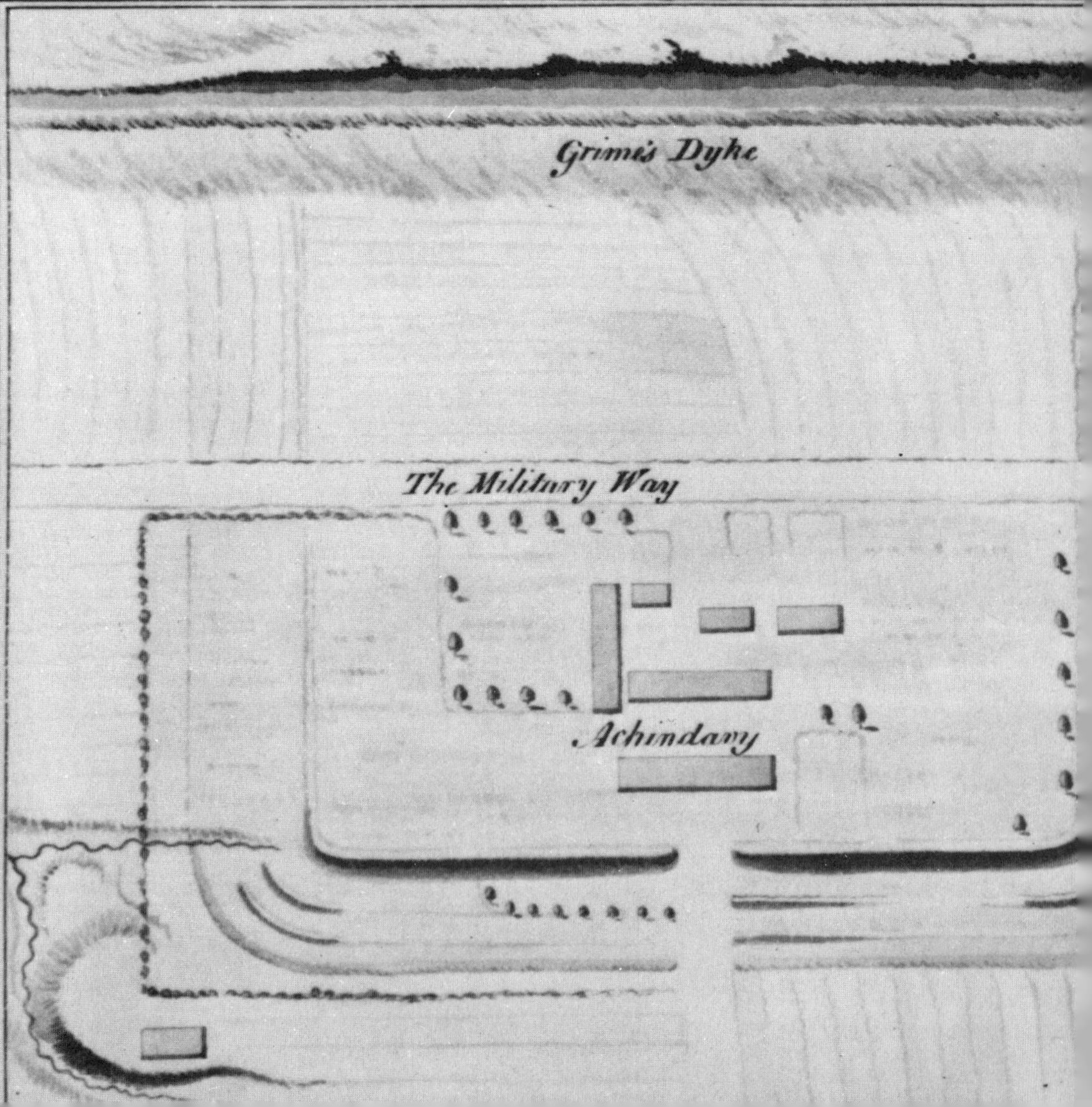

WILLIAM ROY 1726–1790 **PIONEER OF THE ORDNANCE SURVEY**

YOLANDE O'DONOGHUE

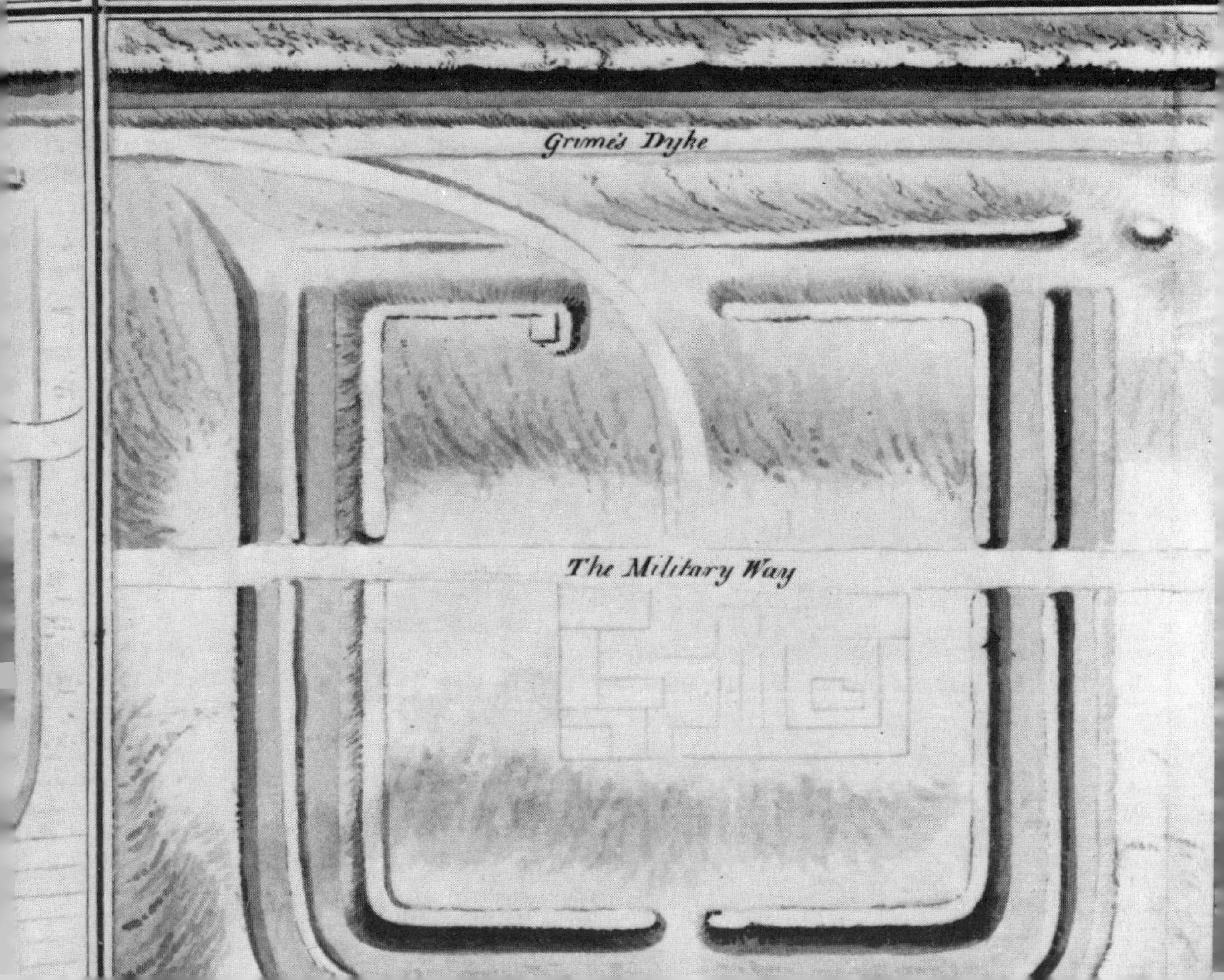

ISBN 0 7141 0387 X
Published by British Museum Publications Ltd.
6 Bedford Square, London WC1B 3RA

British Library Cataloguing in Publication Data

O'Donoghue, Yolande
William Roy, 1726–1790.
1. Roy, William 2. British Library 3. Military engineering–History
I. British Library
016.623'092'4 Z8763.77/

Designed by Roger Davies
Set in Times New Roman and Univers

Printed in Great Britain by
J. W. Arrowsmith Ltd

Contents

Introduction *page 1*

1 The Military Survey of Scotland 1747–55 *page 3*

2 William Roy, Antiquary *page 19*

3 Practitioner Engineer to Major-General 1755–81 *page 30*

4 The National Survey *page 41*

Select Reading List *page 56*

THE BAY
Head of the Mole

The Catalogue

ASPERA

Introduction

On a mild day in April 1784 a group of eminent scientists gathered at King's Arbour on Hounslow Heath to begin the observation of a five mile-long line in the direction of Bushy Park. Now known as the Hounslow Heath base, this line was the foundation on which the first triangulation of Great Britain was built. So began the geodetic operations from which developed the Ordnance Survey. For Major-General William Roy, who was in charge of the proceedings, this was the realisation of a long-standing ambition.

In his life-time Roy achieved national eminence as an antiquary on account of his work on Roman military antiquities. A talented administrator, he followed a successful military career; but it was his outstanding contribution to the founding of the Ordnance Survey which has secured an enduring memorial to his name. As a man he remains an elusive, enigmatic figure. No portrait is known and little has been discovered about the first twenty years of his life or about how he acquired his cartographic skills. Of his work a host of material survives in the form of maps, plans, and military and scientific reports. From this it is possible to form a picture of Roy's public image if not of his private face.

This exhibition, mounted by the Map Library in 1976, the 250th anniversary of Roy's birth, brings together for the first time a rich selection of these items, illustrating Roy's life and career. The most important single source is King George III's Topographical Collection, which came to the British Museum in 1828 and is now preserved in the Map Library of the British Library. Here are to be found the unique manuscript maps of the Survey of Scotland (1747–55), Roy's earliest archaeological plans and drawings, and his later reconnaissance and strategic maps made in the course of his military career. These are supplemented by the fine volume presented to King George III in 1774, now in the King's MSS of the Department of Manuscripts, comprising MS archaeological plans which Roy prepared for his *Military Antiquities of the Romans in North Britain*, published posthumously in 1793.

The British Library gratefully acknowledges the generosity of those who have lent important additional material to the exhibition.

Notable contributions have been made by the Department of Prints and Drawings, and the Department of Coins and Medals of the British Museum. From the Royal Collections at Windsor Castle comes a hitherto unknown early letter from Roy to Lieut.-Colonel David Watson, and Roy's proposal of 1766 for a national survey, which ranks as the most important document in the history of the founding of the Ordnance Survey. Neither of these has been previously exhibited; they are lent by gracious permission of Her Majesty the Queen, together with drawings by the artists Thomas and Paul Sandby. Official files have revealed not only reports and plans made by Roy in his capacity as Deputy Quartermaster-General in the 1760s and 1770s, but also his complete surveying instructions, which were compiled in 1785 for the use of the Engineers and shed new light on the early surveying techniques of the Ordnance Survey. These have been lent by the Public Record Office by kind permission of the Lord Chancellor. The Royal Society has provided copies of significant items relating to the measurement of the Hounslow Heath base and the triangulation of south-east England. Items from the Society of Antiquaries illustrate Roy's work on Roman archaeology, and include an unusual cartoon purported to depict Roy at one of the Society's meetings. A recent discovery has brought to light three of Roy's original army commissions in the Ordnance Survey Offices at Southampton, two of which are displayed in the exhibition. An example of an eighteenth-century barometer has been lent by the Science Museum, London.

The exhibition is arranged in sections reflecting four major themes of Roy's life. The first deals with the Survey of Scotland on which Roy was employed for nine years, 1747–55. During this time he acquired his interest in Roman antiquities, and this provides the theme for the second section, William Roy, Antiquary. Roy's military career from the time of his appointment as Practitioner Engineer in 1755 to his promotion to Major-General in 1781 forms the subject of the third part. This is followed by a final section showing the development of Roy's plans for a national survey, culminating in the triangulation of south-east England.

1 The Military Survey of Scotland 1747–55

William Roy was born on 4 May 1726 at Miltonhead, Lanarkshire (now Strathclyde) in Scotland, where his father and grandfather were factors to the lairds of Milton. He attended Carluke Parish School and then Lanark Grammar School, where he was 'soundly drilled in the elements of Latin and Mathematics'. Unlike his younger brother James, who matriculated from Glasgow University in 1742 to become a clergyman, Roy did not follow any course of higher education. It has been suggested that he might have assisted his father in the preparation of estate plans, and was then employed by the Post Office, perhaps as a surveyor of post roads.

The political unrest in Scotland, generated by Jacobite ambitions to restore the Stuarts to power, culminating in the rebellion of 1745, provided Roy with an opportunity to prove his cartographic abilities. By 1747, a year after the Young Pretender, Prince Charles Edward, had been defeated at Culloden, Roy, although a civilian, had become Assistant Quartermaster to Lieut.-Colonel David Watson, Deputy Quartermaster-General in North Britain. As Roy's map-making was already of a high standard it is surmised that he gained his skill working for several years before 1747 as a civilian draughtsman in the Ordnance Office in Edinburgh. In that year, Watson conceived the idea of making a map of the Highlands; and 'as Assistant Quartermaster [Roy later recalled], it fell to my lot to begin . . . the execution of that map'.

The completion of 'that map', the original objective of which was to assist in the pacification of the Highlands, took nine years from 1747 to 1755. During this time Roy remained a civilian, although subject to military authority, and in the later stages he had men of junior military rank under his command. It may be assumed, however, that Roy was not entirely occupied with the Survey, which was only a part of the general strategy for opening up the Highlands. The quartering of troops, disposition of Commands, general improvement in communications and arrangements for military supplies all came within the purview of a Quartermaster's duties, and would undoubtedly have been undertaken by Roy during his term of office as Assistant Quartermaster. Maps and plans were indispensable aids to such tasks, as illustrated by the plan of Braemar Castle and Barracks and the annotated Elphinstone map.

Of the young men with whom Roy worked in Scotland, two were to become famous. One was Paul Sandby the 'Father of English water colour art'. The other David (later General Sir David) Dundas, was to be acclaimed the most accomplished British tactician of the century. Paul Sandby was an unknown artist at the time, but was already beginning to evolve his special watercolour technique, displayed in an early view of Drumlanrig. As the official draughtsman of the Survey, Sandby must have worked in close collaboration with Roy, and it is probable that the studies which he made of the participants in the Survey, such as David Watson and Howse, would also have included Roy, who may well be the subject of Sandby's early drawing of the 'Young Man sketching', now in private possession. Few examples survive of the many sketches and paintings which Sandby must have made of the Survey in the Highlands. Amongst these a delightful drawing of the surveying party at Kinloch Rannoch and an early etching have hitherto remained unknown, and are exhibited here for the first time.

The chronology of the Survey of Scotland falls into two distinct periods. The first, from 1747 to 1752, saw the completion of the mapping of the Highlands which was conducted solely by Roy for the first two years, with Sandby as draughtsman. The fair copy of the map, an exquisite manuscript in several sheets, seems to be the work both of Sandby, who depicted the hills with consummate skill, and of Roy, whose hand can be traced in the topographical detail and lettering. The second period, from 1752 to 1755, was taken up with the Survey of Southern Scotland, for which new surveyors were recruited, among them David Dundas, who was Lieut.-Colonel Watson's nephew. The finished product of this part of the Survey stands in sharp contrast to its northern counterpart. Its inconsistencies of style and draughtsmanship together with an unfinished appearance reflect the hurried work of several hands, amongst which Roy's may readily be discerned. The Scottish survey was overtaken by the events of the Seven Years War before it could be completed, and before, as Roy commented, 'many of its imperfections' could be remedied. The maps ceased to be working military documents after 1761, when they were passed to King George III's Library. Nevertheless, the Survey of Scotland remains a notable landmark in the history of British cartography. It was the first time that the mainland of Scotland had been systematically surveyed, and this set the pattern for British military surveys in the second half of the eighteenth century, notably the Survey of Canada and the St Lawrence by George Murray (1760–1761), the east coast of North America by Samuel Holland (1764–75), of Bengal by James Rennell (1765–77), and of Ireland by Charles Vallancey (1778–90). Roy's own ideas for a national survey, first formulated in the 1760s, were profoundly influenced by his long experience on the Survey of Scotland. It was, as another of the surveyors, Hugh Debbeig (later a General) commented, 'the greatest work of this sort ever performed by British Subjects and perhaps for the Representations of the Country not to be equaled [sic] in the World'.

1 Roy's Birth and Baptism, 1726

Extract from the Carluke Parish Register of Baptisms.

Photograph by courtesy of the Scottish Record Office

Roy's parents, John Roy, who was factor to Sir William Gordon of Milton, and Mary Stewart, were married in July 1722. His two sisters Grizel and Susanna were born in 1723 and 1728 respectively, and his brother James in 1730.

This extract from the Carluke Parish Register of Baptisms shows the entry for Roy's birth on 4 May 1726 and his baptism, which was witnessed on 12 May by Lockhart of Lee.

2 Miltonhead

Illustration on facing page

Part of Sheet 5 of the Military Survey of Scotland (1752–55).

MS 1:36,000

BL Map Library K.Top. XLVIII.25-1b,c

The only map known to show the location of the house in which Roy was

2 Extract from sheet 5 of the Military Survey of Scotland, showing Miltonhead

Dalserf
Manse
Mauldslie
Dyke
Park of Mauldslie
Bankbrae
Lawbank
Dalbeg
Dalpatrick
Gillbank
Milton
Miltonhead
Sandylandgate
South Miltonhead
Clydesmill
Overtown
Townhead
Sandyholm
Waygateshaw
Thripwood
Between y Hills

born, this part of the Survey of Southern Scotland was probably surveyed and drawn by Roy himself.

3 Roy's Birthplace Today

Triangulation pillar, Miltonhead.

Photograph by courtesy of the Ordnance Survey

The site of Roy's birthplace at Miltonhead is marked by a plaque, incorporated in an Ordnance Survey triangulation pillar. The plaque was unveiled on 4 May 1956 by Major-General Willis, then Director General of the Ordnance Survey. Colonel Edge, Director General 1966–69, stands on his left.

4 The Military Survey of Scotland, 1747–55

Part of Sheet 12 of the Military Survey of Scotland.

MS 1:36,000

BL Map Library K.Top. XLVIII. 25-1b,c

To assist in the pacification of the Highlands after the 1745 insurrection, a survey was proposed by Lieut.-Colonel David Watson, Deputy Quartermaster-General in North Britain under the Duke of Cumberland. Under Watson's direction the Highlands were surveyed in the years 1747–52, in the first two seasons by William Roy, his Assistant Quartermaster, and then by six surveying parties. In the years 1752–55 the Survey was extended southward to the Border by two parties, the western working under Roy, the eastern under David (later General Sir David) Dundas. These surveys were all made at the scale of 1,000 yards to one inch.

A complete set of the maps (originally in 22 rolls, now in 38 sheets) came to the Royal Library after Watson's death in 1761. At some date after 1763 it was lent or given by King George III to Colonel Roy (as he then was). In 1765, on the death of the Duke of Cumberland, the 'original protraction' of Northern Scotland in 84 rolls, which had been in the Duke's possession, also entered the King's Library. The maps in Roy's custody were returned to the King by Dundas in 1792, two years after Roy's death. In 1828 King George III's Topographical Collection, including the maps of the Military Survey of Scotland, came with his books to the British Museum Library, now the British Library.

5 The Battle of Culloden, 1746

A Sketch of the Field of Battle at Culloden 1746. By Thomas Sandby, R.A. (1721–1798).

Pencil and watercolour, a little pen. 30 × 54 cm

Lent by Her Majesty the Queen

Windsor Castle Inventory of Drawings no. 14722

The Battle of Culloden, 16 April 1746, saw the end of the Jacobite uprising of 1745. This final reverse in the fortunes of the Pretender Prince Charles was brought about by a reformed British command in the person of the Duke of Cumberland. Accompanying the Duke was the artist of this view, Thomas Sandby. A young draughtsman from the Drawing Room in the Tower of London, Sandby later became Deputy Ranger of Windsor Forest.

Sandby's task in Scotland was to record in maps and views the disposition of troops and their encampments. In this rapid sketch, probably made on the spot, he shows the two lines of Highlanders on the right, stretching between Culloden Parks in the distance and the walls of Culloden House grounds in the foreground. The three lines of Cumberland's army are to the left.

6 Culloden House

[Sketch of the area around Culloden House] Will. Roy delin! [1746?].

MS 1:36,000 approx. 14×14 cm

BL Map Library K.Top. L.44-1

This undated sketch by William Roy shows Culloden House, where Prince Charles spent the night before the battle. His troops, reduced to 'five thousand starving, dispirited men', bivouacked on Culloden Moor, below the House. The 'Track of Artillery' depicted on the right of the sketch was probably made by the heavy guns of the British Army.

Comparison of this map with the 'fair copy' of the Military Map of Scotland reveals several differences. Many places are omitted or spelled differently on the sketch, whereas settlements are drawn in more detail.

7 Fort Augustus

A Plan of Fort Augustus with the Land Adjacent. [1750?].

MS 1:2,400 approx. 38×46 cm

BL Map Library K.Top.L.14

Fort Augustus was destroyed during the uprising, and served as the Duke of Cumberland's headquarters in May 1746, when rebuilding was in progress. It may be surmised that here the Duke and Lieut.-Colonel Watson discussed ideas for making a map of Scotland, for the Duke and the generals under his command 'found themselves greatly embarrassed for want of a proper Survey of the Country'. On his return to London in July, the Duke obtained authority for the survey to proceed. The young William Roy, as a civilian Assistant Quartermaster, 'commenced the operation in the neighbourhood of Fort Augustus' in 1747, apparently on an experimental basis. By the end of 1748 'the Specimens of his progress were so satisfactory, that it was determined to extend the Survey over the whole of the North of Scotland'. This plan shows Fort Augustus in about 1750, after it had been rebuilt.

8 David Watson (1713?–61)

Illustration p. 11

Col. David Watson. By Paul Sandby, R.A. (1725–1809).

Black and red chalk. 20×15 cm

Lent by Her Majesty the Queen

Windsor Castle Inventory of Drawings no. 14405

David Watson, the date of whose first commission in the army is unknown, became a Lieutenant in the 25th Foot in 1733, and was placed on the establishment of Engineers in 1744. His services at the siege and recapture of Carlisle, 29 December 1745, and at the Battle of Falkirk, 17 January 1746, were rewarded by promotion to the army rank of Lieut.-Colonel. He also took part in the Battle of Culloden and afterwards remained at Fort Augustus to design and superintend the construction of barracks, fortifications and roads in Scotland.

It was at this time, as Roy reports, that Watson, 'being himself an engineer, active and indefatigable, a zealous promoter of every useful

9 View near Loch Rannoch

undertaking . . . first conceived the idea of making a map of the Highlands'. In the ensuing years, until its completion in 1755, Watson had the chief direction of the Survey. He was promoted Major-General in 1759, and when he died in 1761 was still awaiting reimbursement by the Government for the many expenses incurred.

This drawing by Paul Sandby shows Watson at the age of about 35.

9 A Surveying Party in the Field, 1749

Illustration overleaf

View near Loch Rannoch. [By Paul Sandby R.A. (1725–1809), 1749.]

Watercolour and pen and ink. 17 × 24 cm

BL Map Library K.Top. L.83-2

This view by Paul Sandby depicts a surveying party in the field. According to David Dundas 'each Surveyor was attended by a Non-Commissioned Officer and 6 Soldiers as Assistants – One carried the Instrument – Two measured with the Chain. Two for the fore, and back stations – *One* as Batman'. The surveyor in this view is using a circumferentor. Also known at that time as a plain theodolite, this instrument has a graduated circle with compass and alidade. Two soldiers can be seen measuring with a chain, and two with flags to mark the fore and back stations.

A similar drawing in the Pennant Collection, National Library of Wales, bears the incomplete inscription: 'Ramnock [sic] in the Highlands of Scotland 1749, when the military survey . . . '

10 Paul Sandby R.A. (1725–1809)

Illustration overleaf

Paulus Sandby. Ruralium Prospectuum Pictor. Fra^{s} Cotes pinx^{t} E. Fisher fecit. Publish'd according to Act of Parliament 1763.

40 × 29 cm

BM Department of Prints and Drawings, 1904-11-30-2

Paul Sandby, younger brother of Thomas, joined the Board of Ordnance Drawing Room in the Tower in 1741. He presumably accompanied his brother and the Duke of Cumberland to Scotland in 1746, and in 1747 was given the task of preparing the 'original protraction' from the Survey of Northern Scotland. He was also the 'Chief Draftsman of the fair Plan'.

Sandby returned to England in 1751, but was recalled to Edinburgh in 1753 and according to George Chalmers, writing in 1810, 'reduced that immense map, and drew it on a scale of 12,000 feet to an inch with a thousand graces'.

11 Surveying Instruments

Geometrical and Graphical Essays . . . By George Adams.

London: Printed for the Author, by R. Hindmarsh, 1791.

22 cm

BL Department of Printed Books 51.e.9

Published in 1791, and dedicated to Charles Lennox, Third Duke of Richmond and Master General of the Ordnance, this book describes the instruments and methods of surveying and plan drawing of the late eighteenth century. Plate XV depicts different forms of compasses, among which Figure 4 represents a 'small circumferentor, or theodolet' of a kind 'much used by General Roy, for delineating the smaller parts of a survey'. Such a compass would probably have been used on the Survey of Scotland.

8 Colonel David Watson

Reproduced by gracious permission of Her Majesty the Queen

12 Employment of the Troops in Scotland, 1748

Lt. Col. Watsons proposal for encamping and employing the Troops in North Brittain for 1748.

MS 19 × 16 cm

Lent by Her Majesty the Queen

Royal Archives Windsor Castle Cumberland Papers Box 31/10

The Survey of Scotland was only part of the general strategy for opening up the Highlands. Road building and the repair and construction of fortifications were the major projects carried on under the direction of Lieut.-Colonel Watson. Roy wrote in 1785 that 'the rise and progress of the rebellion which broke out in the Highlands of Scotland in 1745, and which was finally suppressed, by his Royal Highness the late Duke of Cumberland, at the battle of Culloden . . . convinced Government of what infinite importance it would be to the State, that a country, so very inaccessible by nature, should be thoroughly explored and laid open, by establishing military posts in its inmost recesses, and carrying roads of communication to its remotest parts'.

This work schedule for the troops in Scotland for 1748 is almost entirely restricted to road building.

13 Braemar Castle, 1748

Ground about Castletown in Braemarr. [By William Roy, 1748.]

MS 1 : 18,000 approx. 21 × 16 cm

BL Map Library K. Top. XLIX. 13-2a

This sketch, probably by Roy, shows the situation of Braemar Castle, which Watson in 1748 planned to repair and convert into barracks. An almost identical sketch, but oriented to magnetic north, is in the National Library of Scotland and is endorsed with the note 'Rec^{d} with the copy of Colonel David Watson's letter to Mr. Skinner [later Chief Engineer] dated 12 May 1748'. The Military Map of Scotland shows Braemar Castle as barracks, suggesting that it was made later than this map, after the repairs to the castle had been completed.

14 Repairs to Braemar Castle, 1748

Plan of Braemarr Castle with the design'd Repairs [and] Plan and Section of Braemarr Castle as it stands at present. [By William Roy, 1748.]

MS 23 × 38 cm

BL Map Library K.Top. XLIX. 13-2b

This plan of Braemar Castle, probably by Roy, shows the improvements necessary to convert the castle into a military barracks. Following the military convention for showing proposed works, a yellow wash on the upper plan indicates sections intended for alteration.

It has been suggested that Roy was a civilian draughtsman in the Ordnance Office before he worked on the Military Map of Scotland. If so, he must have drawn many plans of this type, and such work would also have been consistent with his duties as Assistant Quartermaster while he was employed on the Survey.

15 Elphinstone's Map of Scotland

A New and Correct Mercator's Map of North Britain . . . By In° Elphinstone [with MS annotation] Explanation of the Posts proposed to be occupied by the Regular Troops in the Highlands in Summer 1750, with the particular Districts

of each command. Printed for A. Millar, London, March 6th 1745.
1:800,000 approx. 68 × 54 cm
BL Map Library K.Top. XLVIII.19

This map by John Elphinstone, a Practitioner Engineer, was published on the eve of the Jacobite rebellion. Dedicated to the Duke of Cumberland, it was in frequent use by the military command in Scotland. Illustrating the typical use of a printed small scale map for strategic and administrative purposes, this copy is annotated in MS to show the extent of the seven military districts and the distribution of posts and Headquarters in the Highlands for 1750. The small red numbers on the map correspond with the 'No. of Posts' in the left-hand column of the manuscript table.

The annotation of a map in this way would have been one of Roy's duties as Assistant Quartermaster, and other copies of this printed map in King George III's Topographical Collection (not exhibited) are found with similar MS additions marking military roads. George Chalmers, writing in 1810, ascribed these annotations to the hand of Lieut.-Colonel David Watson, but the writing more closely resembles that of Roy.

16 A Surveyor on the Scottish Survey

Mr. Howse, now the Rev. Mr. Howse, who was on the Survey of Scotland.
By Paul Sandby, RA (1725–1809).
Pen and water colour over slight pencil. 18 × 8 cm
Lent by Her Majesty the Queen
Windsor Castle Inventory of Drawings No. 14416

Paul Sandby was noted not only for his landscapes but also for figure drawing. In March 1746 he had submitted to the Board of Ordnance, as an example of his work, a 'Book of Figures' done in Edinburgh. Howse, the subject of this sketch, was one of seven surveyors employed on the Scottish Survey. The others were Roy, John Manson, Hugh Debbeig, William Dundas, David Dundas (who was Watson's nephew), and Williams. Debbeig and David Dundas were to become Generals, but at the time only three of the seven, namely Debbeig, Manson and Williams, were Practitioner Engineers, the rest being civilians.

In answering Aaron Arrowsmith's queries about the Survey in 1806, General Dundas was to refer to all the surveyors as lieutenants, but as he remarked at the time: 'At the Distance of 50 years, and with no materials for Recollection at hand, very distinct answers do not occur'. Howse became a clergyman after leaving the Survey.

17 Surveying in the Highlands, 1750

[Photographic enlargement of an etching made by Paul Sandby in 1750 of a surveying party in the Highlands.]
BL Department of Printed Books 62.i.17

Sandby's earliest attempts at etching were made while he was in Scotland. Most of his drawings depict subjects other than that of his working environment on the Survey, and this rare view of a surveying party is one of three known to have been made by him.

18 Edinburgh Castle, 1753

East View of Edinburgh Castle. Paul Sandby Delin. et Sculp. London. Printed for Robt Sayer & Hen^{y} Overton, 1753.
29×40 cm
BL Map Library K.Top. XLIX.74-d

Every year the surveyors returned to Edinburgh: 'The summer months were spent in the field, the greater part of the winter ones in Edinburgh, where the work was laid down and finished, and every year it was carried by General Watson to London for H. Majestys Inspection'.

The work of preparing the material for the draughtsmen and of drawing the 'fair copy' and reductions was presumably carried out at the Ordnance Office in Edinburgh Castle, shown in this etching by Paul Sandby.

19 Fort George

Fort George. C. Tarrant Fecit [1755?].
MS 1:4,800 approx. 11×18 cm
BL Map Library K.Top. L.28

Charles Tarrant, later Lieutenant-General Tarrant, author of this plan of Fort George, was one of the three draughtsmen employed on the Scottish Survey. The others were Paul Sandby and J. C. Pleydell (later a Lieutenant-Colonel).

20 Drumlanrig in Scotland

[View of Drumlanrig. By Paul Sandby, R.A. (1725–1890), 1750s?]
Watercolour, pen and ink. 15×41 cm
BL Map Library K.Top. XLIX.54.1c

Sandby must often have accompanied the surveyors in the field, sketching landscapes as well as acting as draughtsman. Designated the 'pioneer of topographical art in England' and the 'father of watercolour art', he was one of the twenty-eight members of the Royal Academy nominated by George III on its formation in 1768.

Receiving many commissions to draw country seats of the nobility and gentry, Sandby here depicts Drumlanrig in Dumfriesshire, then the seat of the Duke of Queensbury, 'who has a noble palace here, magnificently seated on the side of a hill, an immense mass, embosomed in trees'. The River Nith and its flood plain appear in the foreground, together with a 'distant Prospect of the Mountains of Galway'.

A similar view from the drawing by Paul Sandby was engraved as Plate XX in *The Virtuosi's Museum, Containing Select Views in England, Scotland and Ireland*, Drawn by Paul Sandby, London 1778.

21 Roy Reports to Watson, 1752

Illustration overleaf

Letter from Roy to Watson, dated Berwick Upon Tweed Sep^{br}: 20th 1752.
MS 33×40 cm
Lent by Her Majesty the Queen
Royal Archives Windsor Castle, Cumberland Papers Box 44/268

Roy wrote this letter to Watson after the mapping of the Highlands had been completed in 1752, when it was decided to continue the work to cover the south of Scotland. As Dundas recalled: 'The whole line of the coast, and of the Southern Border with England was accurately surveyed and measured by General Roy . . . '.

It is evident that Roy reported on his progress at frequent intervals to

Watson, from whom he received his orders. In this report, the only one known to survive, he apologises for not having written sooner: 'I have been in such a part of the Country, as made it impossible for me to receive or send any Letters'. The report describes, in all the detail required of a military reconnaissance, river courses, fords, roads and bridges of the area, and also reflects Roy's interest in Roman antiquities. He ends: 'I propose surveying a little way round this place [Berwick] tomorrow, and setting out on Friday, on the Survey of the Coast of Leith'.

22 Berwick, 1752

Part of sheet 9 of the Military Survey of Scotland.
MS 1:36,000
BL Map Library K.Top. XLVIII.25-1b,c
Part of Sheet 9 of the Survey of Southern Scotland, in Roy's hand, showing Berwick and the road to Edinburgh. Surveyed in September 1752.

23 The Rough Copy

Original protraction of the Highland Survey (1747–52) Sheet 76.
MS 1:36,000.
BL Map Library K.Top. XLVIII.25-1a
The original protraction, or drawing of the map of northern Scotland, was compiled from observations recorded in the surveyors' note books. According to Dundas 'Each Surveyor kept a field book and a sketch book; in the first he noted the angles and measurements of his stations and also the intersections made from each, with observations. In the second which was of a sufficient size, he delineated his stations and the face of the country on each side'.

No field books appear to have survived, but General Dundas recalled in later years that 'the Courses of all the Rivers and their Branches; of all the principal Roads; and of the Lakes, salt and fresh were followed and measured; as well as such other intermediate and Cross Lines as were found necessary for the filling up of the Country'.

The original drawing shown here is of part of the River Dee with Invercauld estate and Braemar Barracks. The vertical and faint horizontal lines covering the face of the map form 2-inch squares (2,000 yard squares according to the scale), which were drawn for copying, or reducing. The vertical lines are drawn at $\frac{1}{2}$-inch intervals, representing 500 yards on the ground. The route taken by the surveyor on his compass traverse is represented by straight lines connecting observation points, and can be seen following the courses of some of the rivers.

24 The Fair Copy of the Military Survey of the Highlands, 1747–52

Sheet 18.
MS 1:36,000
BL Map Library K.Top. XLVIII.25-1b,c
Writing in 1785, Roy referred to the map of Scotland, sometimes known as 'Roy's Map', as 'rather . . . a magnificent military sketch, than a very accurate map of a country'. He ascribed the deficiencies of the map to the use of 'Instruments of the common or inferior kind'. In spite of inherent errors and distortions, the map is a fine example of a military survey, and

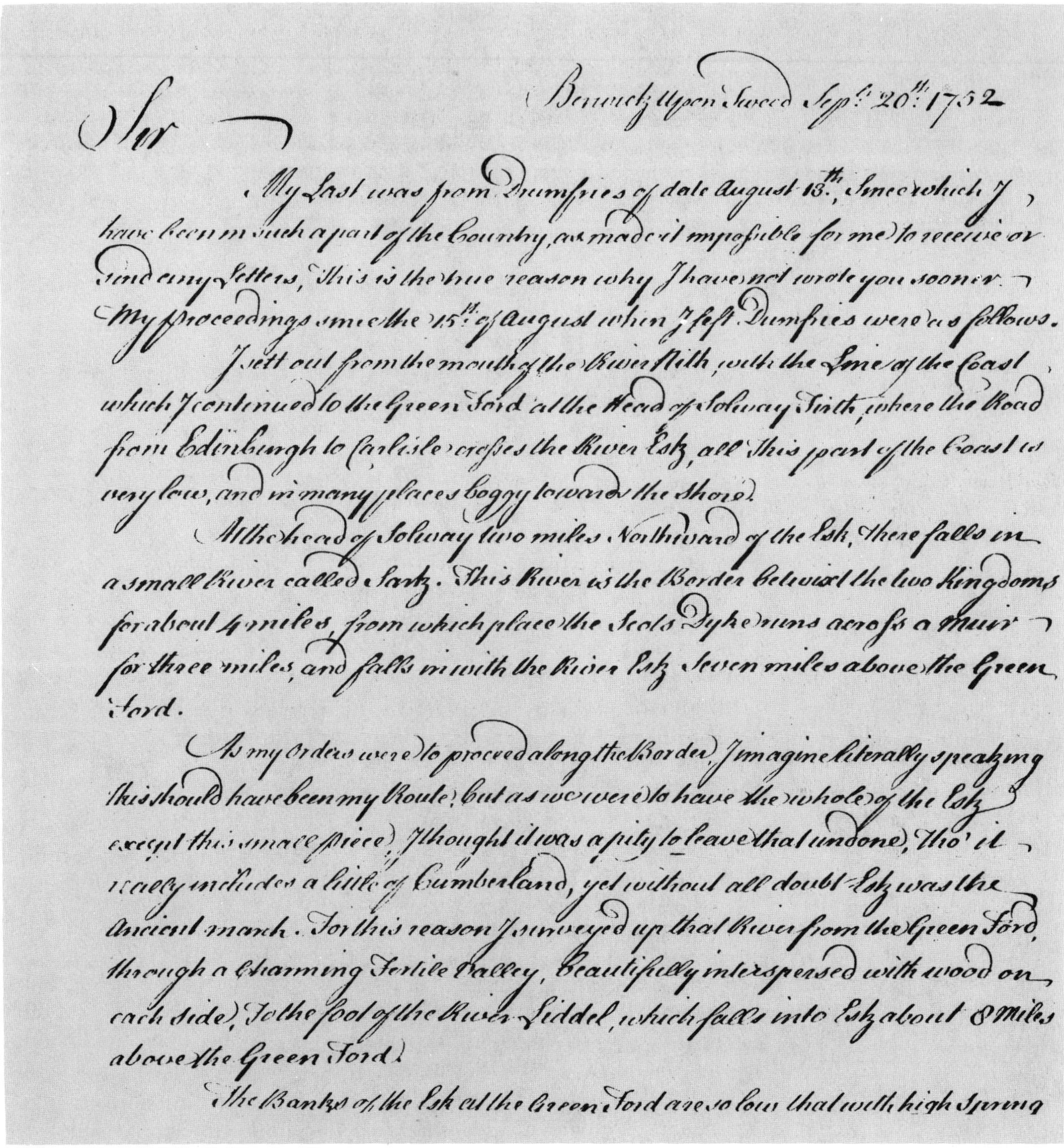

Berwick upon Tweed Sept. 20th 1752

Sir

My Last was from Dumfries of date August 13th, Since which I have been in such a part of the Country, as made it impossible for me to receive or send any Letters, This is the true reason why I have not wrote you sooner.

My proceedings since the 15th of August when I left Dumfries were as follows.

I sett out from the mouth of the River Nith, with the Line of the Coast which I continued to the Green Ford at the Head of Solway Firth, where the Road from Edinburgh to Carlisle crosses the River Esk, all this part of the Coast is very low, and in many places boggy towards the Shore.

At the head of Solway two miles Northward of the Esk, there falls in a small River called Sark. This River is the Border betwixt the two Kingdoms for about 4 miles, from which place the Scots Dyke runs across a Muir for three miles, and falls in with the River Esk Seven miles above the Green Ford.

As my Orders were to proceed along the Border, I imagine literally speaking this should have been my Route; but as we were to have the whole of the Esk except this small piece, I thought it was a pity to leave that undone, Tho' it really includes a little of Cumberland, yet without all doubt Esk was the Ancient march. For this reason I surveyed up that River from the Green Ford, through a Charming Fertile Valley, Beautifully interspersed with wood on each side, To the foot of the River Liddel, which falls into Esk about 8 Miles above the Green Ford.

The Banks of the Esk at the Green Ford are so low that with high Spring

21 Letter from Roy to Watson, Berwick, 20 September 1752

Reproduced by gracious permission of Her Majesty the Queen

provides a valuable record of settlement and land use in eighteenth century Scotland.

The customary colour conventions for military maps of the period are employed: blue-green for water features, green for woodlands, yellow with hatching for land under cultivation, buff for moors, solid red for houses and red outline for formal grounds. The fair copy of the map of the Highlands shows 'the Mountains and Ground . . . shaded in a capital style by the pencil of Mr. Paul Sandby', while much of the detail appears to be in Roy's hand.

25 The Survey of Southern Scotland, 1752–55

Sheet 7.
MS 1:36,000
BL Map Library K.Top. XLVIII.25-1b,c

In 1752 'the Highlands being nearly finished it was determined to extend the survey over the south of Scotland also'. David Dundas joined the Survey at this time and was initially placed under Roy's tuition.

The southernmost part of this sheet was surveyed and drawn by Roy. Writing to Watson in September 1752, Roy said 'As my orders were to proceed along the Border, I imagine literally speaking this should have been my Route, but as we were to have the whole of the Esk except this small piece, I thought it was a pity to leave that undone, tho' it really includes a little of Cumberland'. Roy also used the opportunity to examine the Roman forts south of the border. A note in Roy's hand in the bottom left-hand corner of the sheet describes where the 'Roman Ways crosses the Border'.

This sheet shows the 2-inch copying or reducing squares, numbered in the margins to facilitate identification of any one square. The north and south margins would have been similarly annotated, but appear to have been trimmed from the sheet.

Unlike the Survey of the Highlands, no fair copy of the southern survey was ever made, and only the original protraction remains, numbering nine sheets. In 1755 'the scenes previous to the commencement of the Seven Years War, soon employed and dispersed the several Assistants'.

26a The Reduced Map

[Reduction of the fair copy of Northern Scotland and the original protraction of Southern Scotland. By William Roy. *c.* 1755.]
1:150,000 approx.
BL Map Library K.Top. XLVIII.25-1e, sheets 11 and 14

The only complete reduction of the Scottish Survey to be made, this map, originally mounted as a single roll, is now preserved in 21 sheets. Unlike the 'Great Map' which is oriented to magnetic north, the reduction is oriented to true north. Although there is no direct evidence for the attribution of this map to Roy made in the British Museum catalogue of 1844, the cartographic style bears a striking resemblance to Roy's known work, and there is little doubt that this map is a brilliant example of his exquisite draughtsmanship. Incorporating the Roman sites which Roy had discovered up to 1755, the reduction was probably begun in that year and may have been completed in 1756, when Roy was working with Watson, in whose possession the larger scale map remained until his death in 1761. The reduced map was not amongst Roy's materials which were returned to the Royal Library by Dundas in 1792 after Roy's death, and was probably presented to the King at an earlier date.

26b The King's Road

Part of the Reduction from the Great Map, shewing the Kings Road which is express'd by a Red Line, & the Country Roads by a Brown Line. N.B. The Great Map is 3,000 feet to an Inch, & the Reduction is 1/4 or 12,000. [By William Roy, 1753.]

MS 34 × 23 cm

BL Map Library K.Top. XLVIII.19

This reduced extract of the 'Great Map' was presumably drawn by Roy, although the hills may have been put in by Paul Sandby. This is the only known contemporary map to give the scale of the original survey and drawings. No scale is given on any of the original protractions, nor on the fair drawings of the Military Map of Scotland.

The map of the King's Road was probably made between the years 1753 and 1755, when Paul Sandby was recalled from the south of England to Edinburgh to reduce the Survey of Scotland from the scale of 1 inch to 1,000 yards to 1 inch to 4,000 yards. Sandby's reduction, which is now mounted on one roll measuring 10′ × 7′ (K.Top XLVIII.25-1d), was never completed.

2 William Roy, Antiquary

It is not known when Roy first acquired his interest in Roman fortifications. No doubt his imagination was fired by the similarity between the British military operations to contain the Highlanders after the Jacobite rebellion of 1745, and those of the Romans in checking the movements of the clans in the first two centuries AD. Roy's preoccupation with the vestiges of the Roman invasions first became apparent during the Survey of Southern Scotland, 1752–55. Though the 'study of Antiquity was but little the object of the young people employed in that service', Roy wrote, 'yet it was not wholly neglected, many sketches of Roman works having been made in the ordinary course of the other observations'.

The earliest of these sketches which Roy is known to have made, for example the map of the River Esk and Liddel Moat, date from 1752 when he was surveying the border with England. During the next three years Roy continued to survey and sketch the Roman sites which he discovered in the course of executing the 'Great Map'. He was further inspired by meeting Captain (later Lieut.-General) Robert Melville who was bent on reconstructing the geography of Tacitus' *Agricola*. From Melville Roy learned the structural differences between permanent forts and temporary camps, resulting in his brilliant plans of the Roman remains at Ardoch, contrasting with his earlier misinterpretation of sites such as that at Burnswark. The last season of the Survey of Scotland culminated in the most precise survey ever made of the Antonine Wall at that time. The resulting map is an impressive achievement. At the scale of 1:36,000, it depicts the entire length of the wall together with plans and profiles of the forts.

In 1755 Roy left Scotland to join the army in the south of England. Nearly ten years elapsed before he resumed his archaeological interests in Scotland. His discovery in 1764 of a new site at Cleghorn rekindled his old enthusiasm and in the next decade he collected and made numerous plans and sketches, compiling the material for his *Military Antiquities of the Romans in North Britain*. The volume was eventually published in 1793 by the Society of Antiquaries, of which Roy had been elected a Fellow in 1776.

The greatest contribution of this work to Roman archaeology lay in the magnificent plans of Scottish sites, some of which are no longer visible today. Roy was scrupulous to distinguish between plans made by accurate measurement and those 'done by common pacing only . . . such as were taken after this slighter method are called sketches'. Three sets of Roy's manuscript illustrations are known. The earliest (and least complete) comprises the plans which Roy made while engaged on the Scottish Survey, and which passed into the Library of King George III, together with the second set, prepared between 1764 and 1773. The third collection, almost identical to the second, was bequeathed to the Society of Antiquaries.

27 The River Esk

Plan of Part of the River Esk, with the Plan and Section of a Roman Camp. [By] Will: Roy. Surveyed 1752.

MS 1:37,000 approx. 16×43 cm

BL Map Library K.Top. VI.5

The earliest known plans of Roman military antiquities by William Roy date from 1752, when he was surveying the border country for the Military Map of Scotland. Reporting to Watson in September 1752, Roy wrote, 'I surveyed up that River [the Esk] from the Green Ford, through a charming fertile valley . . . to the foot of the River Liddel, which falls into the Esk about 8 miles above the Green Ford'.

This map depicts the area described in Roy's report and shows the position of the 'Roman Bath' at Netherby, and the 'Moat or Liddels Strength' on the banks of the River Liddel. The map is oriented to the south-east.

28 A Roman Temple at Netherby

Plan of Part of A Roman Temple at Netherby. [By] W: Roy, 1752.

MS 48×31 cm

BL Map Library K.Top. X.63-a

In 1752 Roy described Netherby as 'an old Roman Station . . . situated on a rising ground on the English side'. Showing his eye for Roman architecture, he continues: 'Here I had the pleasure of seeing the Remains of a very curious Roman Temple or Bath, it is not yet entirely discovered, but what is I have made a plan and section of'.

Of the three known states of Roy's plan of the Netherby remains, this appears to be the earliest. In the later variants, which lack any reference to the altar, the title has been altered to read 'Roman Bath' instead of 'Roman Temple'.

29 An Altar to Fortune

This remarkable Alta to fortune was found in the outer Room of a Bath at Netherby, Cumberland. [By William Roy, 1752.]
MS 16 × 10 cm
BL Map Library K.Top. X.63-b

This altar was discovered in the sacrifice room of the Bath at Netherby in 1732. The cult of the Goddess of Fortune demanded that the priest and people be purified by water. The inscription translates as: 'To the Holy Goddess Fortune the Preserver, Marcus Aurelius Salvius Tribune, of the first cohort of the Spaniards called Aelia, and of 1,000 horses, pays his vow willingly and deservedly'.

This sketch was probably made by Roy and is annotated in his 'unofficial' hand.

30 Liddel Moat

Plan of Liddil Moat, A Roman Post Near Netherby on the River Esk. [By William Roy, 1752.]
MS 1:725 approx. 44 × 27 cm
BL Map Library K.Top. X.58

Describing the situation of the fortifications north-east of Netherby, Roy wrote in 1752: 'At Liddel Foot on the English side [of the border] on a steep rocky bank about 80 feet high, there is an old Roman Camp of a semicircular form, strongly fortified with double ditches'.

The earliest of three known manuscript states, this plan was probably drawn while Roy was employed on the Scottish Survey.

31 Birrens Fort

Plan of the Roman Post at Birrens near Middleby Kirk in Annandale. [By William Roy, 1753.]
MS 1:1,600 approx. 28 × 26 cm
BL Map Library K.Top. XLIX.54-2

Drawn by Roy during the Survey of Southern Scotland, this plan was published with slight alterations in his *Military Antiquities, 1793.* The title was altered to 'Plan and Section of the Station at Birrens . . . supposed to be the Blatum Bulgium of the Romans'. Blatobulgium was a Roman head-quarters building at Birrens. Originally erected during Agricola's advance north in AD 81–84, it was the only fort in the Scottish lowlands to be destroyed in the revolt of AD 155, when it was garrisoned by the German reinforcements of the Roman legions. The fort was rebuilt with stone buildings in AD 158; the building shown in this plan is Birrens farm.

32 Burnswark Siege Camps

Illustration overleaf

Plan of Burnswork Hill in Annandale with the Camps & Posts adjoining to it supposed to be the Castra Exploratorum of the Romans.
[By William Roy, 1753.]
MS 1:3,700 approx. 38 × 26 cm
BL Map Library K.Top. XLIX.54.3

This is the earliest of three MS plans known to have been made by Roy to depict the Roman forts now called Burnswark. The site comprises an Iron Age native fort on the summit of the hill, flanked by Roman siege works. The latter were built as practice camps by the Roman army on manoeuvres. The three mounds in front of the northern gates of the southern Roman camp were catapult emplacements, known as the 'Three Brethren'.

Unaware that the buildings were siege works, Roy commented that 'from this remarkable hill [which rose 920 feet above sea level] an army detachment could keep a constant lookout', hence the term *Castra Exploratorum* in the title, and his further inference that 'the very disposition of the camps and posts around this hill shew that the Romans chose not to venture their whole force on one side of it . . . lest the enemy, by surprise, come behind them and obtained possession of the summit'.

This plan was published in Roy's *Military Antiquities of the Romans in North Britain*, 1793, with the title altered to 'Birrenswark Hill . . . supposed to have been occupied by the sixth legion'. The Sixth Legion was stationed in Britain during the reign of the emperor Hadrian, AD 117–138.

33 Roman Camps at Ardoch

Illustration overleaf

Plan of the Roman Camps and Posts near Ardoch in Strathallan. [By William Roy, 1755.]

MS 1:6,000 approx. 34 × 24 cm

BL Map Library K.Top. L.79-2a

This plan showing a permanent post and temporary encampments illustrates Roy's progress in the interpretation of Roman military antiquities. During the Scottish Survey only the permanent, and therefore more prominent, fortifications had been studied and sketched. The larger size and slighter entrenchments of the temporary camps were explained to Roy by Captain Robert Melville, who had been searching for traces of them in Strathmore in 1754. On his return to Edinburgh, Melville described his 'first proselyte' as 'the present Gen. Roy, then one of the surveying Engineers'.

'Knowing now what a temporary camp really was', Roy spent some time in the following summer, 1755, augmenting his collection by 'taking exact plans of those that had been newly discovered'. Among them were the temporary camps adjoining the north of the station at Ardoch, depicted on this plan. Lacking the Latin inscriptions of the later copies, which were annotated in the light of his subsequent studies, the plan derives from Roy's original collection.

34 The Roman Fort at Ardoch

Plan of the Roman Post at Ardoch in Strathallan. [By] Will: Roy, July 1755.

MS 1:1,200 approx. 43 × 24 cm

BL Map Library K.Top. L.79-2b

The fort at Ardoch, shown in this plan from Roy's early collection, is now ranked as one of the most impressive Roman remains in Scotland. Built originally by Agricola during his advance into Scotland, it continued in occupation until the end of the first century. It was then re-occupied in the second century as an outpost of the Antonine Wall.

The 'Roman Military Way from the Post at Strathgeth', shown on the right of this plan, was part of a military road running north from Camelon

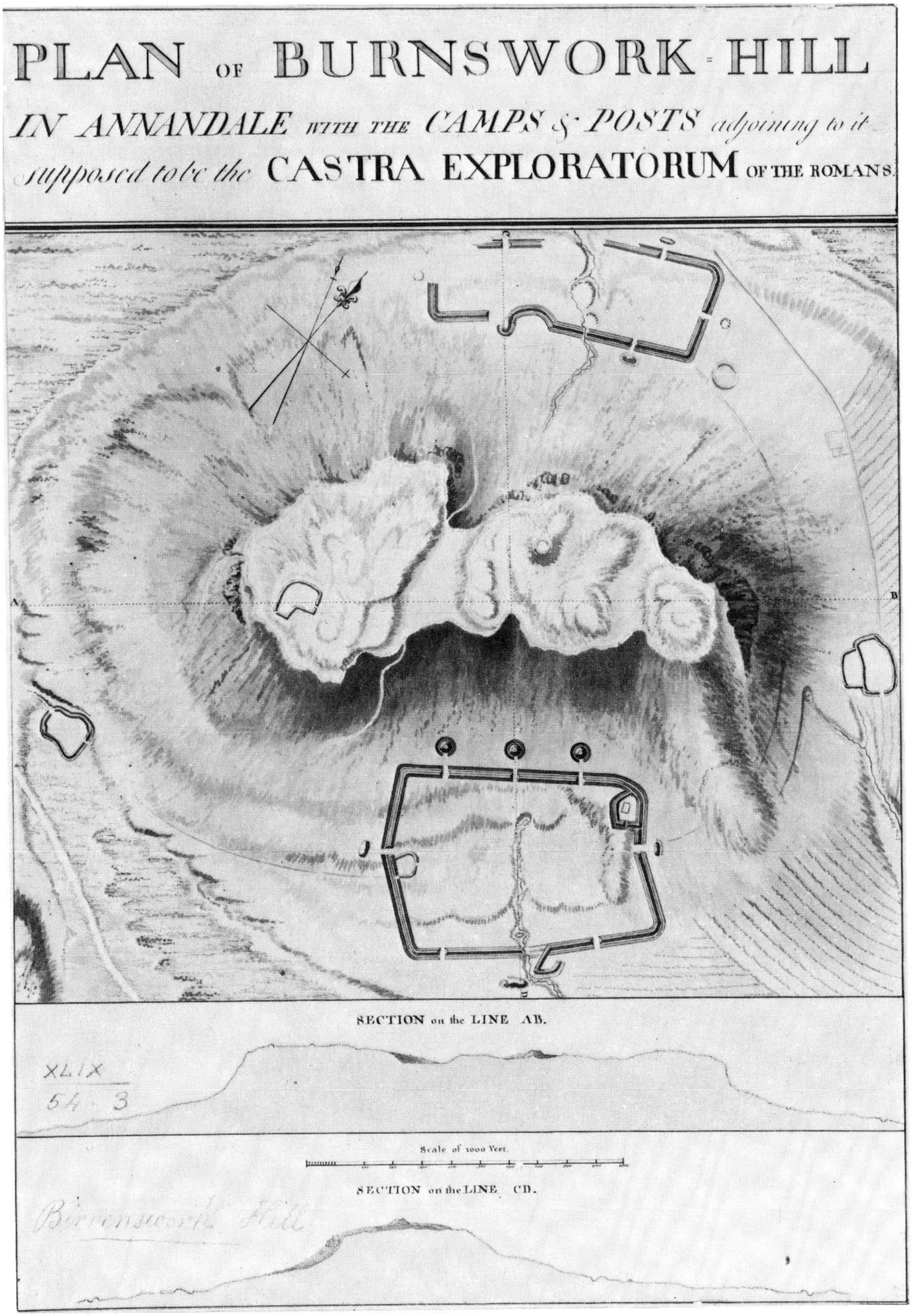

32 Plan of Burnswark Hill

in Stirlingshire to Bertha, a fort on the river Tay, upstream of Perth. Its purpose was to isolate Kinross and Fife from the hostile tribes of the Highlands.

35 Dalginross

Plan of the Roman Camp at Dalginross Near Combrea Kirk in Glen-Earn. Surv^{d} 1755 by Will. Roy.

MS 1:6,000 approx. 37×29 cm

BL Map Library K.Top. L.79-3

After the Battle of Mons Graupius in AD 84, when Agricola's army defeated the northern tribes, forts were built in the main river valleys to guard the exits from the Highlands. Dalginross, on the river Earn, was one of these. It was also the site of a temporary camp, shown here in a plan made by Roy in the summer of 1755.

36 Strathgeath Fort

Plan of the Roman Post at Strathgeth near Inverpeffery in Strathgeth. [By] William Roy, July 1755.

MS 1:2,500 approx. 33 × 26 cm

BL Map Library K.Top. L.83-3

Strathgeath was a frontier post in the Earn Valley, guarding the Roman road from Camelon to Bertha and protecting the area to the north of the Antonine Wall. This plan, like those of Dalginross and Ardoch, was surveyed by Roy in the 1755 field season. It was later published in *Military Antiquities*, 1793, entitled 'Plan and Sections of the Roman Station Hierna near Strathgeth on the River Ern'.

37 The Antonine Wall

Illustration overleaf

Plan showing the Course of the Roman Wall called Grime's Dyke . . . together with Plans of those Stations belonging to the Wall . . . Surveyed in July 1755. In: The Military Antiquities of the Romans in North Britain, Vol. IId, July 1773. [By William Roy]

MS 1:36,000. 53×170 cm

BL Department of Manuscripts King's MS 248.f.43

According to Roy, the Antonine Wall 'was observed in the ordinary way' during the Scottish Survey, but 'without the wall itself becoming the principal object . . . it was therefore judged proper, in 1755, to survey accurately the line of this old intrenchment'.

The Wall was built about AD 140 between the Firths of Forth and Clyde and to act as a base for operations further north; it was abandoned in AD 158. When the plan was ready for publication in 1773, Roy did not attempt to give a detailed description of the Wall in the accompanying text, 'since from a plan of this kind . . . a much truer notion may be obtained . . . of every particular relating to the wall'. He had 'endeavoured to represent the wall and its military way, in the state which they appeared in 1755, making such parts darkest as were then most entire; those lighter that were less conspicuous; and only dotting others where they could barely, if at all, be traced'.

This collection of drawings, together with the first volume of text, was presented to King George III in 1774. In his will, Roy had stipulated that 'if at any time the collection should be published the King's copy would be

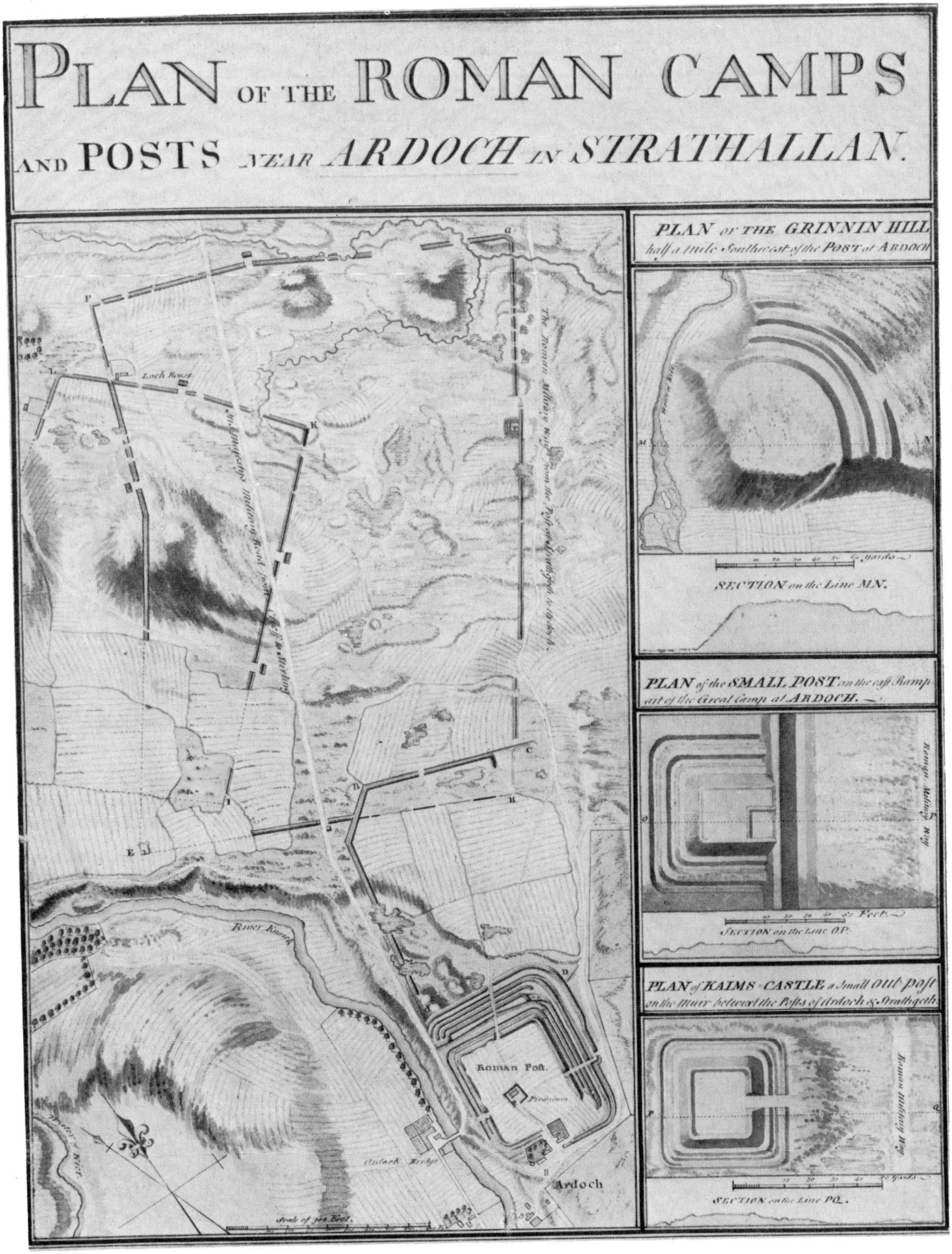

33 Roman camps near Ardoch in Strathallan

best to engrave the drawings from'. In the event the copy used was the less complete second set, which Roy bequeathed to the Society of Antiquaries.

38 A New Discovery, 1764

Plan of the Camp of Agricola at Cleghorn in Clydesdale. Sep^{br} 7th 1764. [By William Roy.]

1:9,000 approx.

Photograph of the manuscript in BL Department of Manuscripts King's MS 248.f.15

In the interval between 1755 and 1764, Roy had become an engineer, seen service in Germany, had achieved the army rank of Major and become Deputy Quartermaster-General of the Forces in South Britain. The search for Roman camps was now a subject 'in a great degree forgotten, and probably would never have been more thought of, had it not been for the accidental discovery of a camp in the south-west of Scotland'.

The camp was at Cleghorn, shown here in Roy's plan dated September 1764. Its discovery immediately revived Roy's old enthusiasm for Roman archaeology, and prompted him to employ others, in his absence on duty in the south, to search for further evidence of the routes of Agricola's advance north. In the next few years, with only occasional visits to Scotland, Roy was to intensify his study of the Roman occupation of the north, reading all available scholarly literature, and compiling materials for his own book.

39 The Real Site of Trimontium

Plan of the Environs of the Eildon Hills, on the south Bank of the Tweed, at the bottom of which, it is supposed the Trimontium of the Romans was situated. [By William Roy, 1771.]

1:50,000 approx.

Photograph of the manuscript in BL Department of Manuscripts King's MS 248.f.29

After five years' absence Roy returned to Scotland via Carlisle in 1769, making sketches of the camps of Torwood Moor, Tassiesholm and Channelkirk. On his journey south to the border after his visit, he was struck with the impressive view of the three peaks of the Eildons as seen from the south. It instantly reminded him of Ptolemy's description of the Roman fort of Trimontium, hitherto believed to be located in south-west Scotland.

His belief that the Eildon Hills were indeed the site of Trimontium inspired him to 'rectify the ancient geography of these parts'. Two years later, in 1771, he examined the locality and found traces of a fort which 'it must be owned, were . . . much too slight to decide absolutely the point in question'. Work on the Edinburgh–Hawick railway in about 1845 finally uncovered the remains of Trimontium, located slightly to the north of the site shown on this plan, just east of Newstead.

40 The Environs of Lanark, 1764

Plan of the Environs of Lanark . . . shewing . . . the situations of the Station at Castle-Dykes and Agricola's Camp at Cleghorn. [By William Roy 1764.]

1:36,000 approx.

Photograph of the manuscript in BL Department of Manuscripts King's MS 248.f.35

The plans made by Roy in 1755 were to be the last of the Scottish sites

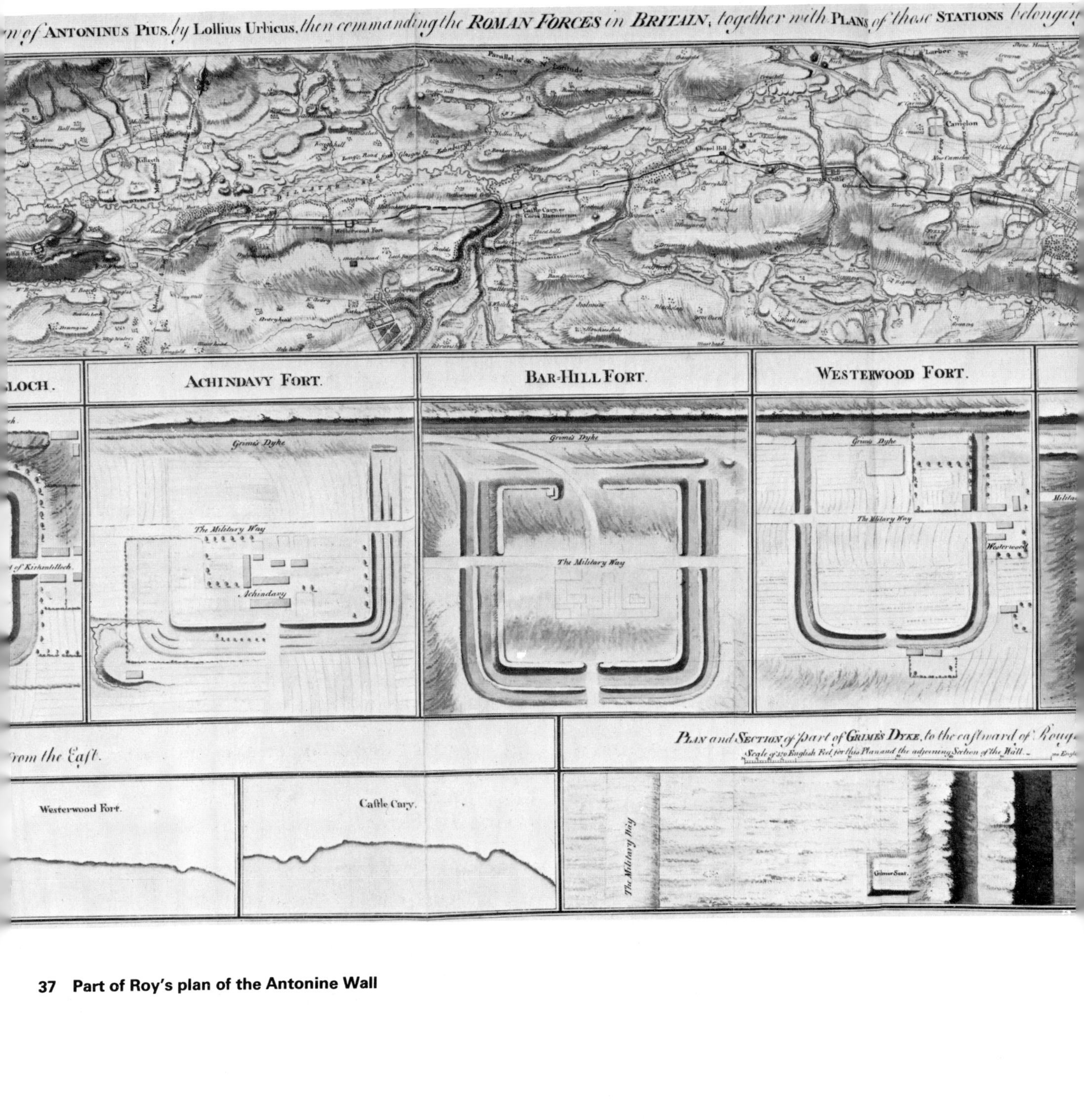

37 **Part of Roy's plan of the Antonine Wall**

depicted for a period of almost ten years. 'Called to the observance of the actual manoeuvres of modern armies, instead of endeavouring to investigate those of the ancients', he was fully occupied with the duties demanded by active service in the Seven Years War, 1756–63.

Roy was back in Scotland in the late summer of 1764, presumably to visit his mother, who had moved from Miltonhead to Lanark after his father's death in 1748. This map, drawn at the same scale as the Scottish Survey, shows the situation of the Roman camp at Cleghorn, situated only a few miles from his mother's home, and discovered during his visit in 1764.

41 Roy's Map of Roman Scotland

Mappa Britanniæ Septentrionalis Faciei Romanæ Secundum Fidem Monumentorum . . . J. Cheevers Sculp^{t} [1773.]

1:1,200,000 approx. 78×54 cm

BL Map Library K.Top. XLVIII.25-1g

This map of Roman Scotland is the only map derived from the Scottish Survey published in Roy's lifetime. It was engraved almost twenty years before the publication of the *Military Antiquities of the Romans in North Britain*, of which it formed the first plate. Showing all the Roman sites known to Roy, it was not entirely superseded until the Ordnance Survey's *Map of Roman Britain* was published in 1924.

This example is the earliest of three known states. The second, engraved in 1774, is distinguished by the inscription 'a G^{mo} Roy Londini 1774' within the cartouche, and the addition of three new sites. In the third state, the words 'Tabulam Hanc Thomas Vincentius Reynolds Gulielmi Roy haeres, Societati Antiquariorum Londinensi D:D.' have been added below the cartouche, indicating a date after Roy's death in 1790.

The only original drawing known, which was exactly followed for the publication of the map in its first state, is to be found in the King's copy of the manuscript, BL Department of Manuscripts King's MS 248.

42 Instructions for the Publishing of Roy's Manuscript

Society of Antiquaries Minute Book. Vol. XXIV, 13–1–1791 to 20–6–1793

55 cm

Lent by the Society of Antiquaries of London

Roy's second manuscript of the *Military Antiquities*, bequeathed to the Society of Antiquaries, was received with great enthusiasm by the Society's Fellows. The 'Introduction' was read as a communication to the Society on 27 January 1791, and, between January and July that year, other extracts were used at a further seven meetings. On 11 April 1791 the decision was made that it be 'recommended that the Council to the Society to direct the publication'.

The entry in the Minute Book for 16 April, 1791, recorded the instructions for printing and publication.

43 The Published Work

The Military Antiquities of the Romans in Britain. By the late William Roy. London, The Society of Antiquaries, 1793.

32 cm

BL Department of Printed Books 460.g.11

Not until the discovery of the camp at Cleghorn in 1764 did Roy contemp-

44 Cartoon, 'The Antiquarian Society'

Reproduced by courtesy of the Society of Antiquaries of London

late preparing his work for publication. Initially to comprise two short essays, the project rapidly enlarged its scope. As Roy observed: 'From small beginnings, it is however, no unusual thing to be led imperceptibly to engage in more extensive undertakings'. The *Military Antiquities* finally consisted of five parts, comprising an abridged history of the Romans in Britain, a history of the Roman militia, a descriptive topography of Scotland, the ancient geography of North Britain and a description of the Antonine Wall. Completed in July 1773, the work was not published until May 1793.

Every contributing Fellow of the Society of Antiquaries, which published the volume at its own expense, was entitled to receive a copy in sheets, which, for an extra four shillings and sixpence, would be half bound.

44 A Meeting of the Society of Antiquaries

Illustration above

The Antiquarian Society. London, Pub^{d} June 1st 1812 by Jones.

18 × 36 cm

Lent by the Society of Antiquaries of London

This cartoon depicts an imaginary meeting of the Society of Antiquaries, with Lord Aberdeen (President 1812–46) in the Chair. Roy was elected a Fellow on 21 March 1776, and although the print was engraved more than twenty years after his death, he has been identified as the man standing third from the right. A military coat with a sheaf of Ordnance papers protruding from the pocket, and a Roman vase on the table, are the clues on which this identification is based.

3 Practitioner Engineer to Major-General 1755–81

Roy was twenty-nine years old when he joined the army. Appointed a Practitioner Engineer in December 1755, he left Scotland to join Colonel Watson in the south of England. Together with David Dundas, Roy accompanied Watson as he toured the country from Dover to Milford Haven, reconnoitring the coastal areas in preparation for the expected French invasion. From this period date Roy's many road and reconnaissance maps, of which an early example depicts the route and army camp sites between Guildford and Canterbury.

The Seven Years War (1756–63) provided Roy with his only experience of active service. Following the unsuccessful expedition against Rochefort in 1757 under Sir John Mordaunt, Roy went on to take part in the Battle of Minden in 1759. His printed plan of the battle, used in the subsequent trial of Lord George Sackville, is the only surviving document of the many sketches, plans and notes which he made at this time and eventually bequeathed to David Dundas. Evidently distinguishing himself in Germany, Roy was appointed in quick succession Captain in the Engineers (1759), Deputy Quartermaster-General of the British Forces in Germany (1760), Major of Foot and Deputy Quartermaster-General of the Forces in South Britain (1761) and Lieut.-Colonel in the army (1762).

Throughout his military career, which spanned thirty-five years, Roy held office in a dual capacity. In his lifetime he was best known within the military profession for his close connection with the Quartermaster-General's Department. Roy's design for the wells at Amersham Camp, which he signed as Assistant Quartermaster in 1757, shows that he was employed at an early stage in this kind of work, for which his experience on the Scottish Survey well qualified him.

From 1765 to 1781 he compiled numerous reports on strategy and troop deployments such as that on the Chatham Lines. Many of these were accompanied by maps, for example, that of south-east England, which Roy evidently preferred to draw himself rather than delegate the task, as was customary, to a draughtsman or subordinate officer.

Roy must have been a familiar figure at the Quartermaster-General's Office at the Horse Guards for many years. But he was also an Engineer employed by the Board of Ordnance, and his headquarters would have been the Tower of London. As an Engineer Roy was concerned with surveying and the construction and maintenance of fortifications. In this capacity he was required to submit technical plans such as those of Portsmouth Dock and general reports of defences like those of Gibraltar to the Master General of the Ordnance.

Thus the double responsibility of an Engineer on the one hand, and Deputy Quartermaster-General on the other, occupied Roy for twenty years after the end of the war with France in 1763. Fifteen years elapsed before he became a Colonel in the army in 1777, and this was followed in 1781 by his promotion to Major-General. In 1786, Roy succeeded General Parslow as Colonel of the 30th Regiment. He evidently took a great interest in his regiment and was 'universally liked and respected'. His leisure time was spent in archaeological pursuits and he devoted six years to scientific experiment 'to obtain a Rule for Measuring Heights with a Barometer'.

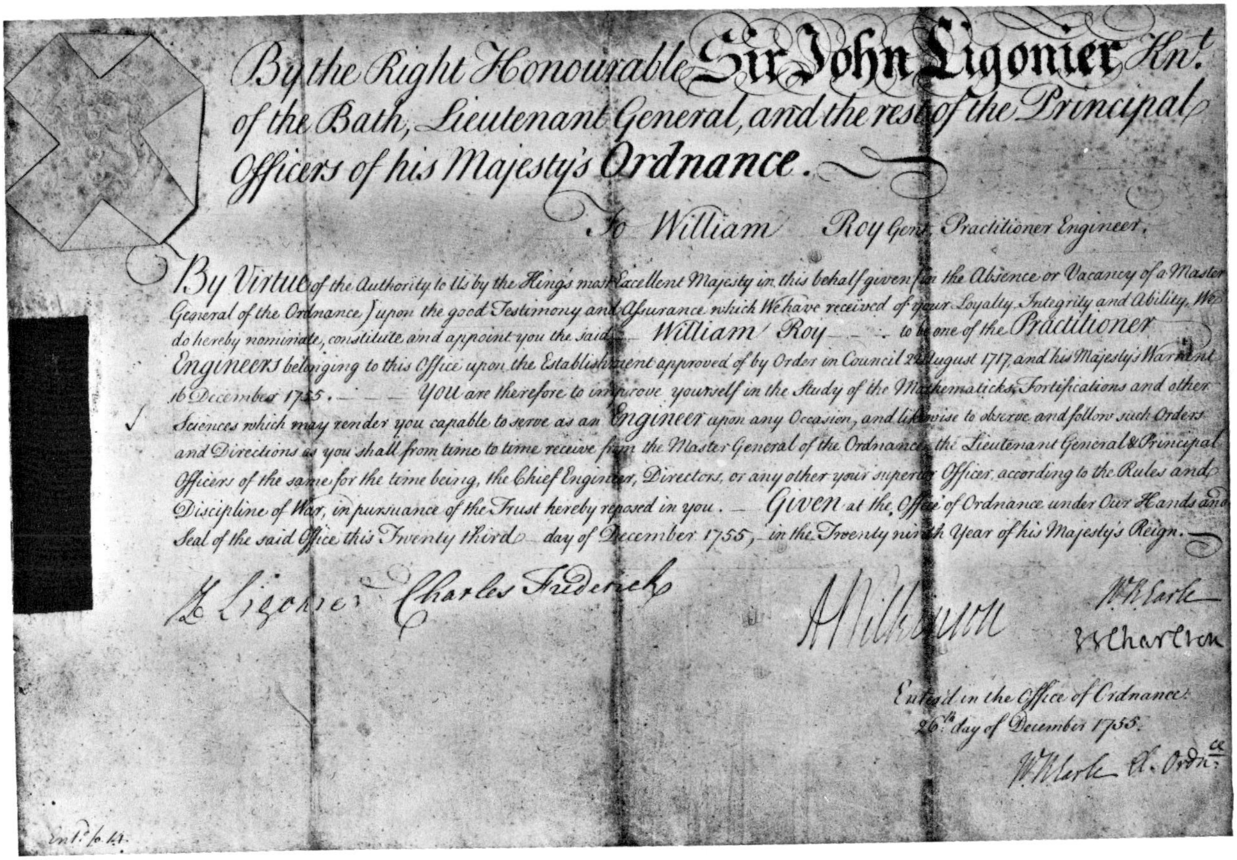
By the Right Honourable Sir John Ligonier Knt. of the Bath, Lieutenant General, and the rest of the Principal Officers of his Majesty's Ordnance.

To William Roy Gent. Practitioner Engineer,

By Virtue of the Authority to Us by the King's most Excellent Majesty in this behalf given (in the Absence or Vacancy of a Master General of the Ordnance) upon the good Testimony and Assurance which We have received of your Loyalty, Integrity and Ability, We do hereby nominate, constitute and appoint you the said William Roy to be one of the Practitioner Engineers belonging to this Office upon the Establishment approved of by Order in Council [illegible] August 1717, and his Majesty's Warrant 16 December 1755. You are therefore to improve yourself in the Study of the Mathematicks, Fortifications and other Sciences which may render you capable to serve as an Engineer upon any Occasion, and likewise to observe and follow such Orders and Directions as you shall from time to time receive from the Master General of the Ordnance, the Lieutenant General & Principal Officers of the same for the time being, the Chief Engineer, Directors, or any other your superior Officer, according to the Rules and Discipline of War, in pursuance of the Trust hereby reposed in you. Given at the Office of Ordnance under Our Hands and Seal of the said Office this Twenty third day of December 1755, in the Twenty ninth Year of his Majesty's Reign.

Ligonier Charles Frederick

Entd. in the Office of Ordnance 26th day of December 1755.

46 Roy's appointment as Practitioner Engineer

Reproduced by courtesy of the Ordnance Survey

45 Quebec, 1775

Plan de la Ville de Quebec . . . Exactly copied by Will: Roy. April 1755.

MS 28 × 35 cm

BL Map Library K.Top. CXIX.33

Drawn in April 1755 while Roy was engaged on the Scottish Survey, but before he became a Practitioner Engineer, this map is typical of the work performed by civilian draughtsmen in the Board of Ordnance. It was presumably made in the Ordnance Office in Edinburgh as one of several copies of maps and plans of strategic places in Canada and Europe specially prepared shortly before the outbreak of the Seven Years War.

46 Roy's Appointment as Practitioner Engineer, 1755

Illustration above

By the Right Honourable Sir John Ligonier . . . Lieutenant General, and the rest of the Principal Officers of his Majesty's Ordnance. To William Roy Gent. Practitioner Engineer . . . Twenty third day of December 1755.

28 × 40 cm

Lent by the Ordnance Survey

On completing the field work of the Scottish Survey in the early autumn of 1755, Roy was no doubt occupied in finishing the manuscript map when the prospect of war with France led him to seek his first military employment.

Appointed a Practitioner Engineer at the age of twenty-nine on 23 December 1755, Roy was commissioned Lieutenant in the 53rd Foot less than a fortnight later, on 4 January 1756. This rapid promotion would be justified by his valuable experience in Scotland and his age (Practitioner Engineers were normally ten years younger). Promotion in the Ordnance Corps was, on the other hand, a slow procedure, and Roy did not become a Lieutenant in the Engineers until 1759.

This appointment as Practitioner Engineer, equivalent in rank to Ensign, exhorts Roy to improve himself 'in the study of the Mathematicks, Fortifications and other Sciences which may render you capable to serve as an Engineer upon any Occasion'.

47 Reconnoitring the South of England

Sketch of the Country, betwixt Guildford and Canterbury. As Reconnoitred by Lieut. Col. Watson . . . Drawn by William Roy P: Eng[r] [1756].

MS 1:63,360 approx. 51 × 217 cm

BL Map Library K.Top. VI.103

Roy's first employment on becoming a Practitioner Engineer was to accompany Colonel Watson and David Dundas on a reconnoitring tour of southern England in preparation for the expected French invasion. Working under the 'Orders and Instructions to be observed by Col. Watson's Assistants in Reconnoitring', Roy made several reconnaissance maps during 1756 and 1757; this sketch of the road from Guildford to Canterbury is an early example.

After two years' surveying in England, together with nine years' experience on the Scottish Survey, Roy had acquired an unrivalled knowledge of military mapping on which he was to draw for his future plans for a national survey. From Watson, his Commanding Officer both in Scotland and England, Roy had learned 'that in Military Maps nothing should ever be represented at Guess or Random', and that 'the space of one quarter of a mile truely laid down is more useful than an Imperfect and loose Representation of an entire Country'.

48 Maiden Castle

Plan of the Maiden Castle near Dorchester. Feb[ry] 11th 1757. [By] Will: Roy.

MS 1:2,400 approx. 45 × 56 cm

BL Map Library K.Top. XII.20

Taking time off from his reconnaissances in the south of England with Colonel David Watson, Roy's continuing interest in archaeology led him to make this plan of Maiden Castle with a skill described by Sir Mortimer Wheeler as 'beyond the average of the day'. No written description by Roy of the site is known to survive.

49 Amersham Camp, 1757

Illustration facing page

Design for the Framing and Windlasses &c of the Wells at Amersham Camp. May 30th 1757. [By] William Roy Assis[t] Qua Ma[s].

MS 38 cm

Lent by the Public Record Office WO 30/119

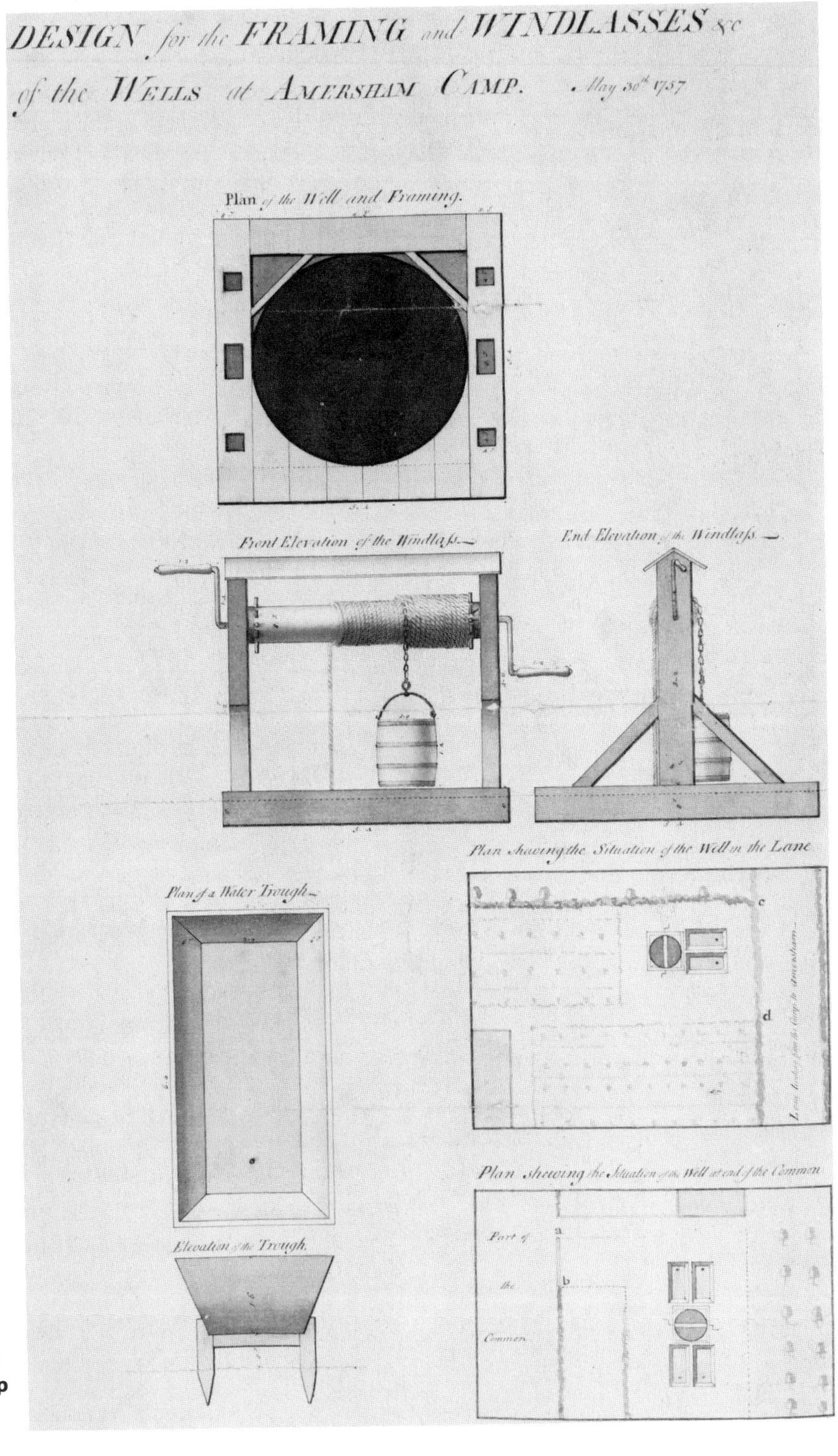

49 Design for the Framing . . . of the Wells at Amersham Camp

Reproduced by courtesy of the Public Record Office

Roy's work in southern England in the mid-1750s was not confined to surveying. These plans and designs for the wells at Amersham Camp, together with an estimate of their cost, were drawn up by Roy while he was apparently acting as Assistant Quartermaster, a position for which his experience in Scotland would have well qualified him.

50 Louisbourg

Plan of the Harbour and Fortifications of Louisbourg . . . The Harbour survey'd by Phi. Durrell, & the Fortifications by Willm Henry Bastide. Drawn by L^{t} W: Roy. [1758.]

MS 1 : 7,300 approx. 54 × 76 cm

BL Map Library K.Top. CXIX.90

Originally one of the strongest French bases in North America, guarding the entrance to the Gulf of St Lawrence, Louisbourg was captured by New England colonists in 1745. In that year this large fishing port was surveyed by Philip Durell and Henry Bastide. Restored to France in 1748, the town was recaptured by the English under General Jeffrey Amherst in 1758, presumably the year in which Roy made this copy of the earlier survey.

51 Roy gives Evidence at a Court Martial

The Proceedings of a General Court-Martial . . . upon the Trial of Lieutenant General Sir John Mordaunt. Published by Authority. London, 1758.

20 cm

BL Department of Printed Books 1414.b.35

Planning an attack which would 'speedily and essentially annoy and distress France', King George II appointed Sir John Mordaunt Commander-in-Chief of an expedition against Rochefort on the west coast of France in August 1757. Ordered to 'burn and destroy . . . all docks, magazines, arsenals and shipping', Mordaunt was unable to carry out his instructions owing to inadequate intelligence regarding the approaches and defences of Rochefort.

Summoned before a board of general officers on his return to England, Mordaunt was tried for disobedience of the King's orders, but was subsequently acquitted. Roy, who had accompanied the Engineers on the expedition, was one of many officers called to give evidence at the trial at which he was questioned on artillery and the feasibility of constructing certain fieldworks.

52 The Battle of Minden, 1759

Illustration overleaf

To Prince Ferdinand of Brunswick, This Plan of the Battle of Thonhausen . . . taken from an Actual Survey, is . . . dedicated by William Roy. Survey'd and Drawn by Capt William Roy. Engraved by Thos Major. London, Feby 29, 1760.

1 : 35,000 approx. 61 × 67 cm

BL Map Library 30520.(1)

Serving in the campaigns of the Allied Army in Europe under Prince Ferdinand of Brunswick, Roy was present at the Battle of Minden on 1 August 1759, when the Allies regained the town from the French. His map of the battle came to be published probably as a consequence of the proceedings against Lieut.-General Lord George Sackville, who during the battle had refused to obey the orders of the Prince. Published on 29

February 1760, the day when Sackville's court martial opened, 'the plan of Lieut. Roy so much relied on' was evidently specially printed for the occasion and played a prominent role in the trial.

53 Roy, Deputy Quartermaster-General

George the Third . . . To Our Trusty and Welbeloved William Roy . . . appoint You to be Deputy Quarter Master General to Our Forces in South Britain, and to take your Rank as Major of Foot . . . Eleventh day of November 1761.

31 × 42 cm

Lent by the Ordnance Survey

Rising from the rank of Assistant Quartermaster, a post held from the age of twenty-one when employed on the Scottish Survey, Roy was promoted in 1761 (aged thirty-five) to Deputy Quartermaster-General of the British Forces in Germany under the Marquis of Granby.

His administrative talent was further recognised by this appointment to the post of Deputy Quartermaster-General of the Forces in South Britain, dated 11 November 1761, together with promotion to the rank of 'Major of Foot'. His commission as Lieut.-Colonel in the army followed soon after, on 23 July 1762.

54 The Defence of South-East England, 1765

General Map of the Southeast Part of England 1765. [By William Roy.]

MS 1:200,000 approx. 102 × 104 cm

BL Map Library K.Top.VI.97

Appointed on 19 July 1765 to 'inspect, survey and make Reports from time to time of the State of the Coast and Districts of the Country adjacent to the Coast of this Kingdom', Roy spent much time acquiring a 'general knowledge, of the principal Positions and Posts, which an Army should occupy, when occasionally employed for their Security and Defence', as shown in this map of south-east England.

'In laying down the Sketch or General Map', wrote Roy in the accompanying report of 17 July 1765, the 'Positions or Camps represented by streight lines' were strategically placed 'where the several great Roads . . . to the Capital do cross the Rivers or Ranges of Hills'. Conscious of what might be 'defective with regard to the expression of the Ground', Roy explained that 'an Attempt is made at the bottom of the Map, to represent something of the General Section of the Country'.

The map also reflects Roy's interest in Roman military history. 'The Roman Roads and names of Stations', he wrote, 'are distinguished in Red, as likewise ye places of the most memorable Battles'.

55 The Military State of South-East England, 1765

Military Description of the South-East Part of England. London, July 1765. [By] Will: Roy.

MS 41 cm

BL Map Library C.7.d.12

This report 'on the nature of the Country . . . in the neighbourhood of the Capital', was largely compiled from the observations, maps and sketches which Roy had made in the 1750s while reconnoitring with Colonel Watson. Divided into three parts, the report describes the 'remarkable Ranges of Hills' in the vicinity of London, the principal positions to be

52 *Illustration overleaf* **Part of map of the Battle of Thonhausen**

march'd toward Lubecke, where the Enemy abandon'd his Posts the next Morning. The same Day (the 27th) the Battalion of Buck
with the Brigade of heavy Artillery of the Left, took a Camp in the Rear of the Grenadiers.

The 28th Gilsae's Regiment joined the Army, from Stolzenaw.

The 29th the Army march'd in 3 Columns, by the Right, from Petershagen Camp, to that of Hille. His S. H. Duke Ferdinand led the 1st Column, compos'd of the first Line; the heavy Artillery conducted by Count La Lippe Buckenburg, form'd the 2d Column; and Genl. Sporcken led the 3d which consisted of the second Line. The Army took it's Camp between Hille and Fredewald, having the Villages of Nord Hemmeren and Holthausen in it's Front; the head Quarters were at Hille, and cover'd by the Regiments of Napier and Kingsley. A Disposition was made of the Piquets of the Army; the British were posted in the Village of Hartum, at L, the Hanoverian in Sud Hemmeren at M, the Hessian in the Wood between Hartum and Holthausen, at N, those of Brunswick in Stemmeren, at O, and the Piquets of the Cavalry in the Woods, at P, with a Detatchment upon the Road from Hartum to Hahlen, at Q. —— The 2 Brigades of light British Artillery, assign'd to the Piquets; and the Generals of the Day were order'd to Hartum. —— In order to conceal the March of the Army, Genl. Wangenheim's Corps was formed under Arms, near the Batteries, Count Buckenburg had erected before Thonhausen; and when those Troops went back to Camp, the Regiment of Buckenburg, with the Brigade of heavy Artillery of the left Wing, encamp'd in the Front of the Line. —— This Day His S. H. desired all the General Officers to inform themselves, very exactly, of the several Passages and Routs, through which the Army was to march, into the Plain of Minden, and to make themselves perfect in them, in case the Army shou'd be order'd to advance.

The 30th in the Afternoon, the 3 Battalions, of Linstow, Prince Charles, and the first of Behr (Brunswick) march'd from Camp, under the Command of Genl. Gilsac, to take Post at Lubecke, where they were joined the next Day, by a Detatchment of 300 Horse of the right Wing.

The 31st in the Afternoon, His S. H. renewed his Orders, to all the Generals who were to lead the Columns, to examine in Person, those Routs, which their respective Columns were to take, in order to get into the Plain of Minden; and particularly to examine the Ground, between the Windmill of Hahlen, and the Village of Stemmeren; where the Army was to form in Order of Battle, according to the Line mark'd RR.

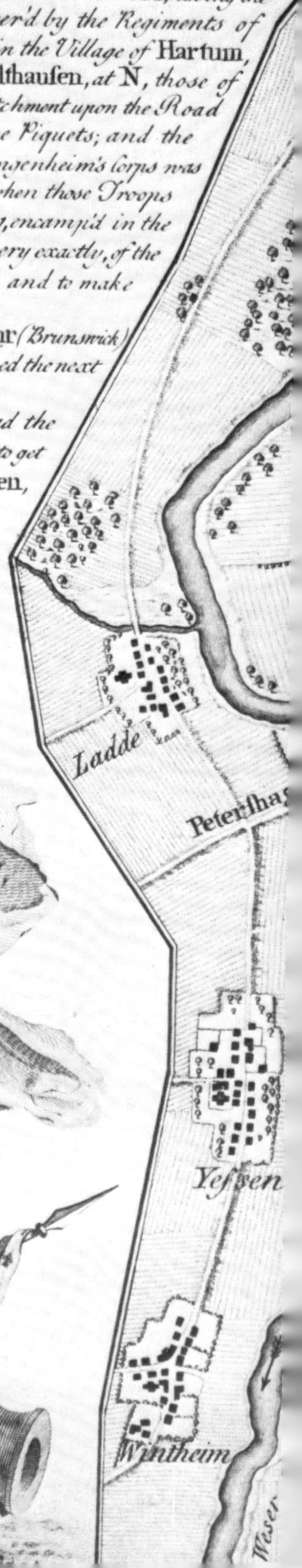

Camp traced for the Army
Swart Zum Breit Wind Mill
Vort Meyer
Petershagen Wood
Grenadiers 17 July
Wangenheim's Corps 16 July
Mesling
Camp of the Army 16 July
Peter shagen Heath
Halle
Offenstede
The Troops of the differen
British Troops
Hanoverian
Cavalry
Infantry
Grenadiers
Artillery

taken up by the army in case of invasion, and also provides a historical résumé of past invasions of Britain. Another copy of the 'Military Description' of south-east England in King George III's Library, 75.k.7., is dated 17 July 1765.

56 A Visit to Ireland, 1765

General Description, of the South Part of Ireland. London July ye 24th 1766. [By] Will: Roy.

41 cm

BL Department of Printed Books 75.k.5

Roy visited southern Ireland in August 1765 to collect military intelligence regarding its topography, communications and natural resources. This 'imperfect account' compiled from 'slight and cursory observations only' was intended, as Roy wrote, to point out 'what seems most remarkable in the nature of the Ground and wherein the situation and present state of the Forts, near the principal Towns and Harbours appear to be defective'.

57 Ireland, 1765

General Map of the South Part of Ireland . . . From observations made in August 1765. [By William Roy.]

MS 1:400,000 approx. 106 × 105 cm

BL Map Library K.Top. LI.30a

This 'general Sketch of the Country' of Ireland was drawn by Roy to illustrate the written report of his visit in August 1765. Spending only three weeks in Ireland, Roy had not found time to 'take any measures or observations relative to the geographical parts'. For this reason he described the Sketch as 'only enlarged from the common Maps . . . by the representation of the principal Ranges of Hills, and some other particulars in the ground' which he was careful to emphasise 'were all drawn by the eye'. Likewise, in describing the 'principal Harbours, laid down at the bottom of the Map', he stressed that their scales were merely 'by way of giving a general idea of the proportion that takes place', yet he continued, 'measurements by these scales cannot be dependent upon as just'.

58 Portsmouth Fortifications

Sections and Profils of the Design for Fortifying Portsmouth Dock. [By] Will: Roy Eng^r^ [1770.]

MS 54 × 186 cm

Lent by the Public Record Office MR 925(2)

Drawn by William Roy in his capacity as Engineer rather than as Deputy Quartermaster-General, this drawing of the fortifications at Portsmouth was probably made to accompany his report of 1770. The lines of the three sections and ten profiles depicted in this scheme for fortifying Portsmouth Dock are located on an accompanying map of the harbour, PRO MR 925(3) (not exhibited) which, although not signed by Roy, was evidently also made by him.

59 View of Gibraltar

59 Gibraltar

Illustration above

A View of the South Part of the Mountain of Gibraltar. Taken by Lieut.-Gen[l] Skinner His Majesty's Chief Engineer of the Garrison in 1740. Drawn by William Test 1779.

MS 55 × 146 cm

BL Map Library Maps 184.g.2.(11)

'In 1768 he seems to have visited Gibraltar' states the Dictionary of National Biography entry for Roy. Yet in his report on the 'state of the works' at Gibraltar, dated 16 June 1769, Roy wrote that he had not had 'an opportunity of examining things upon the spot' and that consequently his account would 'therefore of course have no farther weight, than as it is found consistent with the General Rules of the Science . . . '.

Evidently his visit, if he made one, was not concerned with the fortifications of Gibraltar. Roy's report was probably compiled from maps, documents and views of Gibraltar such as this example by William Test, copied in 1779 from an earlier drawing of 1740, at the beginning of the French and Spanish siege which was to last until 1783.

60 Experiments with Barometers, 1771–77

Mr. Ramsden's portable barometer. From 'Experiments and Observations made . . . for measuring Heights with a Barometer'. Royal Society, *Philosophical Transactions*, LXVII pt. II, 1777.
28 cm
BL Department of Printed Books L.R. 292

The diversity of Roy's scientific interests is illustrated by his work on measuring heights with barometers, described in a paper read to the Royal Society in 1777. His experiments, made during the five years from 1771 to 1776, took him as far afield as Schiehallion in Scotland and Snowdon in Wales. He was assisted in the operations by Joseph Banks, Charles Blagden and Dr Lind, prominent Fellows of the Royal Society, of which Roy himself had been elected a Fellow in 1767.

Shown here is a portable barometer by Jesse Ramsden, used by Roy and consisting of a 'simple straight tube fixed into a wooden cistern'. Roy evidently formed his own collection of scientific instruments, for barometers were to be found among his books, maps and mathematical instruments auctioned by Christie's after his death in 1790.

61 Portable Barometer

Mountain barometer. Made by West. *c.* 1790.
Lent by the Science Museum London Inv. 1893-134

Specially adapted for portability, this closed cistern mercury barometer was frequently used for measuring altitudes. A thermometer showing Centigrade and Fahrenheit scales is placed near the top of the barometer, which is graduated in inches and is read by a vernier index. The wooden case enclosing the lower part of the tube is also graduated in inches, serving as a rough measuring rod.

62 Army Encampments 1781

Report concerning the Positions for an Army in front of Chatham Lines, between them and Sittingborne. April 18th 1781. [By] Will. Roy DQMG.
33 cm
Photocopy of the manuscript in the Public Record Office WO 30/115

During the years of the American War of Independence (1775–83), Roy, in his capacity as Deputy Quartermaster-General (a post which he held until his death in 1790), made many reports on defensive troop deployment in southern England.

One of his duties was that of quartering armies; and in this report, written six months before his promotion to Major-General on 19 October 1781, he enumerates the advantages and drawbacks of potential camping sites between Chatham and Sittingbourne. Callums Hill, for example, which 'commands an extensive prospect of Sheerness', could be hired for less than £3 an acre, 'a price much more moderate than the highly cultivated Fields by the side of the great Road'. Against the advantage that it was a 'cheap camp', Roy comments that 'the communication to it from all sides are so very bad as to render it impossible to carry heavy artillery to it'.

4 The National Survey

Roy made his first comprehensive proposal for a national survey in 1763, soon after he returned from the campaigns in Germany. Emphasizing Britain's vulnerability to foreign invasion, he stressed the necessity of preparing a plan of defence 'during times of peace and tranquility'. Such a plan would require an accurate knowledge 'at least of the Nature of the Coast, and the principal Positions and Posts which an Army should occupy'. For Roy, the only method of acquiring this information was to make a 'good Military Plan or Map of the whole Country'. Roy's suggestions for a 'general Survey of the whole Island at the public cost' were evidently considered seriously by the government of the day. With Roy as its Director, the Survey was to incorporate the topographical details of the earlier Scottish Survey. The scheme was finally dropped on the grounds that it 'would be a Work of much time and labour, and attended with great Expence to the Government'. Undeterred, Roy submitted a modified proposal in 1766 which was also rejected. Still preserved in King George III's papers at Windsor Castle, only this later document has survived, constituting the first written specification for a national survey of Great Britain.

The subject was not officially raised again in the twelve years which elapsed before the outbreak of war with America in 1775. Meanwhile, Roy still 'entertained hopes that a work which seemed to merit the attention of the public, would, at some future period, be begun'. After peace was declared in 1783, Roy used his spare time to begin a small triangulation of the London area to determine the positions of notable landmarks in relation to the Royal Observatory at Greenwich. He was writing up his observations for the Royal Society (of which he had been elected a Fellow in 1767), when Cassini de Thury, Director of the Paris Observatory, submitted a paper to George III suggesting the triangulation of south-east England. This, connected to the French network, would provide a means of establishing the relative positions of the Greenwich and Paris Observatories. The paper was forwarded to Sir Joseph Banks, President of the Royal Society, who immediately proposed that Roy should take charge of the project.

It was a task for which Roy had been preparing himself for twenty years. 'In the course of my ordinary military employments', he wrote, 'I have not failed to observe . . . such situations as seemed to be the best adapted for the measurement of the bases for the formation of the great triangles'. The measurement of the Hounslow Heath base was completed in 1784 and gained Roy the Royal Society's Copley Medal for Science. Realising that surveying instruments of the requisite precision did not exist, Roy saw that it was necessary to 'reinvent them all', and commissioned Jesse Ramsden to construct, among other devices, a new theodolite. Three feet in diameter and weighing 200 lb, it was eventually delivered to Roy in 1787, after many frustrating delays, and the triangulation was completed in 1789.

Roy's health had deteriorated by 1789 and was not improved by a six-month visit to Lisbon in the winter of that year. He returned to his military duties in London in April 1790, and died suddenly on 1 July. Roy left £8,000 and the freehold of his house in Argyll Street to his heirs. His legacy to the nation was the foundation of the national survey which he had laid down in the six years before his death. He had set out the procedure for accurate triangulation in three lengthy papers published in the Royal Society's *Philosophical Transactions* for 1785, 1787 and 1790. He had procured the expensive equipment and instruments essential to such an undertaking and secured the participation of the Duke of Richmond, Master General of the Ordnance, who had freely made available men and machinery when they were required to assist in the operations.

Roy's triangulation of south-east England was essentially limited in scope, since its purpose was purely to establish the geographical positions of the Greenwich and Paris Observatories. But Roy firmly believed that it presented an unprecedented opportunity for 'extending different serieses [sic] of Triangles . . . in all directions to the remotest part of the Island', thereby providing the best foundation 'for an accurate Survey of the British Dominions'.

In 1791, eleven months after Roy's death, the Duke of Richmond placed the triangulation on a formal footing under the auspices of the Board of Ordnance, and the work was continued with a new measurement of the Hounslow Heath base in 1791. The objective was now 'A General Survey of the Kingdom' to be carried on 'by Government, under the direction of the Master General of the Ordnance'. Roy did not live to see the beginning of the national survey which he had persistently advocated for over a quarter of a century, but had he done so, he would undoubtedly have been its first Director.

63 Roy's Proposal for a National Survey, 1766

Illustration on facing page

Considerations on the Propriety of making a General Military Map of England, with the Method proposed for carrying it into Execution, and an Estimate of the expense. [By William Roy] 1766.

MS 38 cm

Lent by Her Majesty The Queen, George III Papers 415(2)

In this document, one of the most significant in the history of the origins of the Ordnance Survey, Roy in 1766 draws up proposals for a military map of England. It is a modified version of an earlier scheme, discarded for financial reasons in 1763, when 'it came for the first time under the consideration of Government, to make a general survey of the whole island at the public cost'.

The plan of 1766 provided for the incorporation of existing county surveys; the surveying of a 'serieses [sic] of Triangles along the Coast, and along the remarkable Ridges of Hills and principal Rivers'; and the employment of military personnel. Recommending 'an Inch or an Inch and a quarter to a mile' as a 'good scale', Roy anticipated the one-inch to a mile scale adopted in the 1790s for the national survey.

Estimating six to eight years for the completion of the map, Roy calculated its cost at £20,000. The project was not taken up and was soon overshadowed by the war with America in the 1770s.

Considerations on the Propriety of making a General-Military-Map of England, with the Method proposed for carrying it into Execution, & an Estimate of the Expence.—

Tho' the Situation of Great Britain, as an Island, separated from the rest of Europe by the Sea, & protected by the most powerful Navy in the World, are great & Singular Advantages peculiar to Her alone, from which there is reason to hope, that She will never have much reason to dread, in times of War, from the Efforts, even of Her most powerfull Neighbours — Yet when it is considered, that in order to defend her extensive Colonies, this Navy, which is her principal and almost only Security, must be distributed into various distant parts of the World, and that even that Division of it, destined for the protection of her Native Coasts, may at some unlucky & critical period meet with unforeseen Disasters, from an unexpected Attack of the Enemy, or from the effects of Storms, Tempests or Fire; In such circumstances, it cannot be denied but that it may be possible for an Enemy to land, and indeed without any of these unlucky Accidents happening, contrary Winds alone, may put it out of the power of the Fleet, to prevent an Enemy's disembarking in some one particular part or other of the Coast.—

This landing being supposed to be made good, & the Country being entirely without Fortresses; The last resource must be in the Bravery of the Army in particular, & the Inhabitants (whether Militia or others) in general, in opposing the Enemy in the Field, by laying hold of such natural Strengths as the Situation of the Country afforded them, in order to stop the Invaders progress in advancing towards the Capital.—

And

63 Considerations on the Propriety of making a General Military Map of England

Reproduced by gracious permission of Her Majesty the Queen

64 The London Base of 1783

For the Improvement of the Plan of London and its Environs. From *An Account of the . . . Trigonometrical Survey of England and Wales.* By William Mudge and Isaac Dalby. Vol. I. London, W. Faden, 1799.
1:63,360 approx. 35×48 cm
BL Map Library Maps Ref. G.2b

On the conclusion of peace with America in 1783, Roy spent the summer of that year in London on official business. 'I embraced the opportunity', he wrote, 'for my own private amusement, to measure a base . . . across the fields between Jews-Harp . . . and Black Lane near Pancras'. The base, shown on this plan of the 1787 triangulation of the London area, was the foundation of a triangulation carried out 'for determining the relative situations of the most remarkable steeples, and other places in and about the capital . . . and the Royal Observatory at Greenwich'.

Hoping that his enterprise might 'serve as a hint to the public, for the revival of the now almost forgotten scheme of 1763', Roy was recording his results when Cassini de Thury put forward his proposal for a triangulation of south-east England to establish the relative positions of the Paris and Greenwich Observatories. Roy readily accepted Sir Joseph Banks's suggestion that he should undertake the triangulation for the Royal Society.

65 A Rough Estimate of the Cost

Letter from William Roy [to Sir Joseph Banks]. Argyll Street, Nov. 28, 1783.
24 cm
Photocopy of the manuscript in the Royal Society DM 4.f.4

Roy's first task on accepting the work of the triangulation of south-east England was to prepare an estimate of cost. In this letter to Sir Joseph Banks, written from his home in Argyll Street, Roy considers that for 'so laudable a purpose', Government would 'not surely grudge to give the Society £1,000'.

The estimate, which fell far short of the final expenditure of over £2,000, provided for 'Mathematical Instruments of the best kinds', a carriage on springs for their transportation and the 'pay of six men for sixty days . . . at 2^{sh}6^{d} each'.

66 Joseph Banks (1743–1820)

Joseph Banks Esqr, painted by Sir Joshua Reynolds. Engraved by W. Dickinson, Publish'd Jany the 30th 1774 by W. Dickinson and Jefferys and Faden.
56×42 cm
BM Department of Prints and Drawings 31-5-20-54

Famous botanist and natural historian, Banks (later Sir Joseph Banks) was elected a Fellow of the Royal Society in 1766, two years before he accompanied Captain Cook on his first voyage to the Pacific (1768–71). Roy himself became a Fellow of the Royal Society in 1767 and was evidently on friendly terms with Banks by 1775. In that year Banks formed a small, select dining club which met weekly and of which Roy was a member, attending 99 of the 141 dinners held until the club's dissolution in 1784. No doubt this dining club provided a forum for the discussion of Roy's ideas on a national survey and, as President of the Royal Society from 1776 until his death in 1820, Banks was in an influential position to suggest Roy as the person best qualified to undertake the triangulation of south-east England, proposed by the French in 1783. 'The respectable and very worthy President of the Royal Society, ever zealous in the cause of science', took a keen interest in the measurement of the Hounslow Heath base. Roy later recalled that Banks, 'with that liberality of mind which distinguishes all his actions, ordered his tents to be continually pitched near at hand' where onlookers could partake of 'elegant refreshment'.

67 The Hounslow Heath Base, 1784

Plan shewing the situation of the Base measured on Hounslow Heath in Summer 1784. From *An Account of the . . . Trigonometrical Survey of England and Wales.* By William Mudge and Isaac Dalby. Vol. I. London, W. Faden, 1799.

1:16,000 approx. 23×65 cm

BL Map Library Maps Ref. G.2b

It is reported that King George III, a 'generous and beneficient Monarch', Patron of the Royal Society, 'soon supplied the funds that were judged necessary'; and the triangulation began on 16 April 1784 with the measurement of the Hounslow Heath base. Roy had selected the site with more than the immediate project in mind. The base would be well situated, he considered, 'for extending different serieses of triangles from there in all directions to the remotest parts of the Island', leading to an 'accurate survey of the British Dominions'.

The length of the base was finally established at the end of the summer as 27,404.72 feet. 'There never has been so great a proportion of the surface of the Earth measured with so much care and accuracy', declared Roy.

68, 69 The Base Terminals, 1976

Photograph of the north-west terminal, London Airport, Heathrow.
Photograph of the south-east terminal, Roy Grove, Hampton.

In Roy's time the Hounslow Heath base terminals were marked by wooden pipes, a foot in diameter, with a bore of four inches. They were found to be decayed on the remeasurement of the base in 1791, and were replaced by guns. Selected from those unfit for service at Woolwich, the guns were placed vertically, muzzle upwards, with wooden plugs fixed in the bores. Marked with a centre dot, the plugs were covered by iron caps screwed over the muzzle.

At the suggestion of Sir Charles Close (Director General, Ordnance Survey 1911–22), bronze plates were fixed to each of the guns in 1926, to mark the bicentenary of Roy's birth. Summarising the events leading to the base measurement of 1784, the plates were engraved with the inscription 'He [Roy] conceived the idea of carrying out the triangulation of this country and of constructing a complete and accurate map, and thereby laid the foundation of the ORDNANCE SURVEY'.

Formerly in King's Arbour Field, four miles west of Hounslow, the north-west terminal gun was removed in 1944 to make way for airport extensions, and was placed in front of the temporary Headquarters of the Ordnance Survey at Chessington. Returned to Heathrow in 1968, it remained in the Engineering Department of the British Airports Authority until 1972, when it was restored to its original position, grid reference TQ

077767. The south-east gun has remained in its original position, TQ 137709, and can be seen in Roy Grove, Hampton.

70 Roy's Account of the Base Measurement 1785

An Account of the Measurement of a Base on Hounslow Heath by Major-General William Roy F.R.S. & A.S. Read from April to June 16, 1785.
33 cm
Photocopy of the manuscript in the Royal Society Letters and Papers Decade VIII No. 153

Always ready to exploit an opportunity to promote his ideas of a national survey, Roy prefaced his account of the measurement of the Hounslow Heath base with a long statement on the 'great public utility' of 'accurate surveys of a country'. Read to the Royal Society on several occasions between April and June 1785, his paper was published in the *Philosophical Transactions*, Vol. LXXV, 1785, and contained a detailed description of the methods and instruments used. The base had been measured three times with painstaking care with Ramsden's hundred-foot chain, using deal rods twenty feet long and with glass rods, also by Ramsden.

Awarded the Copley Medal of the Royal Society for his unique achievement in precise measurement of length, Roy was judged to have performed 'a labor sufficient to derange a more than common degree of perseverance'.

71 The Copley Medal 1785

The Royal Society Copley Medal for Science
BM Department of Coins and Medals, Miss Banks Collection

William Roy, 'this very skilful engineer' was presented with the Royal Society's Copley Medal for Science (founded on the legacy of Sir Godfrey Copley), on 30 November 1785, for the 'accurate and satisfactory manner in which he has measured a base, for operations of Trigonometry, upon Hounslow Heath'. Sir Joseph Banks, describing Roy's work in his presentation address, referred to Roy as the 'one Person at least' whom 'we possess in this Island . . . willing to undertake and able to execute, the most dificult [sic] operations of mensuration'.

Roy's own Copley Medal apparently no longer survives. This example was presented to William Hamilton in 1770.

72 Roy's Surveying Instructions 1785
Illustration on facing page

General Instructions for the Engineers to be employed in Surveying the Coast and Districts of the Country near it. [With an] Appendix containing practical observations on Surveying. [A copy in Roy's hand of his 'instructions', approved by the Duke of Richmond 17 July 1785.]
MS 33 cm
Lent by the Public Record Office WO 30/115

The most significant document on survey methods known to have been written by Roy, this comprises a set of surveying instructions issued with the authority of the Master General of the Ordnance, and probably intended for use by the Engineer Company. This company, which was founded in 1784 on the reorganisation of the Corps of Engineers and designated the 'Surveying and ready for Field Service', had Roy, then a Lieut.-Colonel in the Corps, as its Commanding Engineer.

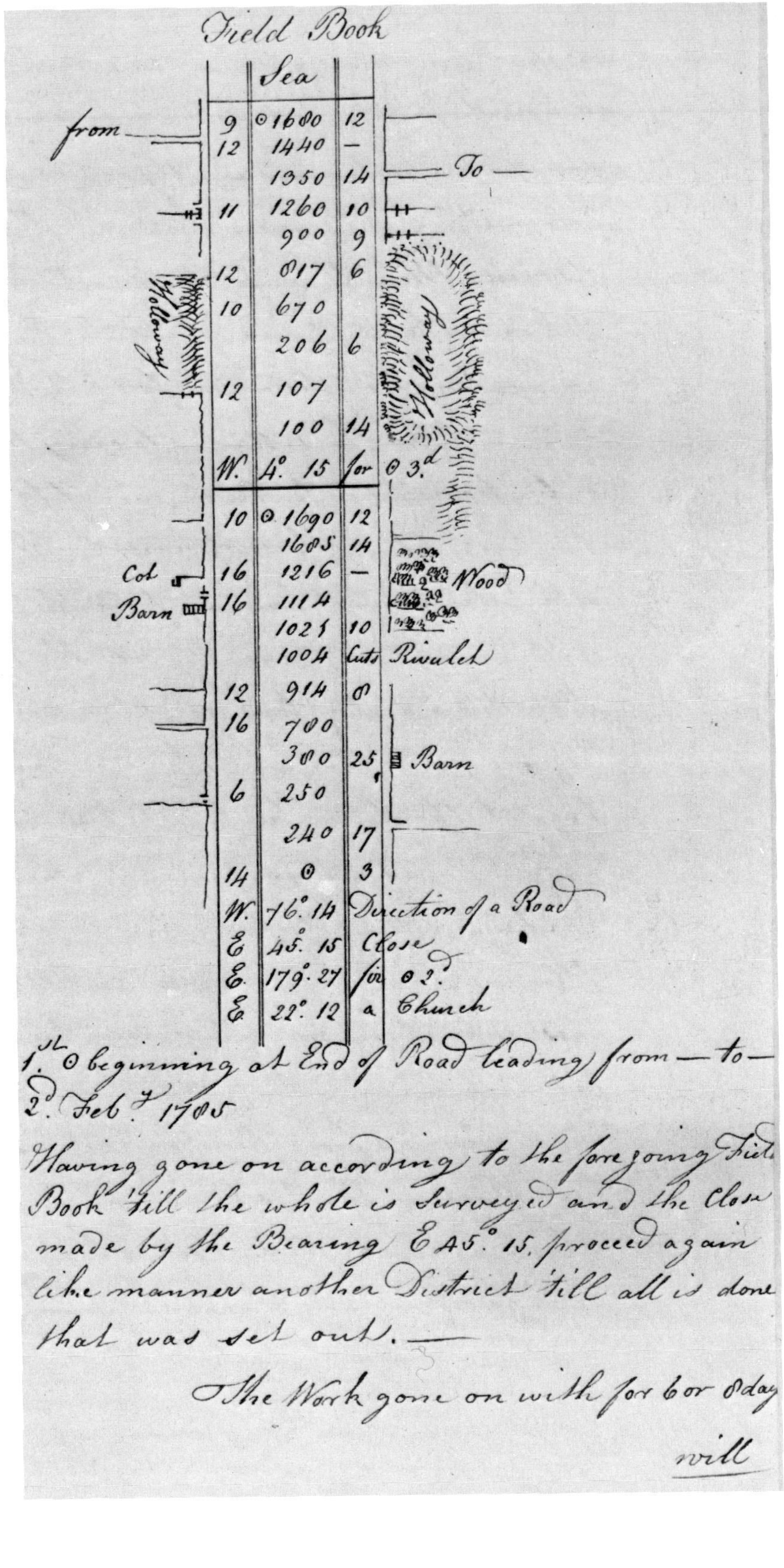

Field Book

	Sea	
9	⊙ 1600	12
12	1440	—
	1350	14
11	1260	10
	900	9
12	817	6
10	670	
	206	6
12	107	
	100	14
W.	4°. 15	for ⊙ 3d
10	⊙ 1690	12
	1605	14
16	1216	—
16	1114	
	1021	10
	1004	Cuts Rivulet
12	914	0
16	700	
	300	25 Barn
6	250	
	240	17
14	⊙	3
W.	76°. 14	Direction of a Road
E	45°. 15	Close
E.	179°. 27	for ⊙ 2d
E.	22°. 12	a Church

1st ⊙ beginning at End of Road leading from — to —
2d Feby 1785

Having gone on according to the foregoing Field Book till the whole is Surveyed and the Close made by the Bearing E 45°. 15. proceed again like manner another District till all is done that was set out. —

The Work gone on with for 6 or 8 day

will

72 Part of Roy's notes on keeping a field book

Reproduced by courtesy of the Public Record Office

Reviewing such topics as the choice of bases, triangulation, instruments, and the organisation of surveying parties, Roy reiterated his choice of the one-inch scale, proposed more than twenty years before, not only for a 'whole County' but also for the 'Island in general', thus pursuing his plan for a national survey. Giving a detailed account of the techniques of topographical survey or 'filling in the triangles' the Appendix, shown here, illustrates the method of keeping field books and advises the surveyor to 'follow the footways if possible as there will be the less Umbrage given to the proprietors of the lands you go through'.

Roy's 'Instructions' distilled forty years' surveying experience. Written while the paper on the Hounslow Heath base was in preparation, they no doubt helped Roy to crystallise his thoughts on the general survey which he saw as an essential tool in national defence.

73 Ramsden's 100ft Steel Chain

For the Account of the Measurement of the Base of Verification with the Steel Chain, in the Autumn of 1787. From *Account of the . . . Trigonometrical Survey of England and Wales.* By William Mudge and Isaac Dalby. Vol. I. London, W. Faden, 1799.

20 × 45 cm

BL Map Library Maps Ref. G.2b

The steel chains which had proved so reliable on Hounslow Heath in 1784 were used again for the measurement of the 'Base of Verification' on Romney Marsh, conducted under the direction of Lieutenant Fiddes of the Corps of Engineers in the autumn of 1787, two months after the triangulation had commenced. The length of the base, deduced from that of Hounslow Heath, had been given as 28,533.3 feet. It remained to be tested by actual measurement.

On completion of the work in December 1787, Roy proudly wrote to his friend Dr Lind 'that our trigonometrical operation answers to a wonderful degree of exactness'. The final computation of the Romney Marsh base agreed with the original calculation to 'within less than a foot'.

Ramsden's 100ft steel chain was supported by complex machinery consisting of specially constructed posts, deal coffers to hold the chain, and elaborate systems of brass scales and pulleys, shown in this diagram. Its manufacture was beset by delays, causing Roy to grumble that 'the apparatus for the measurement of the base with the steel chain, notwithstanding the urgency of the case, was not sent to its destination until the end of the first week in October'.

74 The Steel Chain

Photograph of the 100ft steel chain used by Roy in 1784 and 1787.

By courtesy of the Science Museum London

Ramsden's 100ft steel chain was used for the first experimental measurement of the Hounslow Heath base in 1784; the definitive measurement was made using the glass rods. So impressed was Roy with the performance of the chains that they were used exclusively for the measurement of the Romney Marsh base in 1787.

75 Roy Censures Ramsden

An Account of the Trigonometrical Operation, whereby the Distance between the Meridians of the Royal Observatories of Greenwich and Paris has been determined. By Major General William Roy, F.R.S. and A.S. 1790.

32 cm

Photocopy of the manuscript in the Royal Society Letters and Papers Decade IX No. 168

Frequently accused by Roy in private correspondence of being 'remiss and dilatory', Jesse Ramsden, instrument-maker extraordinary and a Fellow of the Royal Society, is here publicly censured for the serious faults in the chain apparatus used on Romney Marsh in 1787. 'If the maker had not been very negligent', Roy remonstrated, the defect 'might easily have been prevented'.

Roy's paper on the triangulation of south-east England, which was read to a meeting of the Royal Society in February 1790, contained many derogatory references to Ramsden. Protesting strongly to the Council of the Royal Society, Ramsden caused the offensive passages to be deleted from the manuscript draft of the paper. In this example, Roy's strictures on the steel chain equipment are struck out.

76 Ramsden Replies

Extract from a letter by Jesse Ramsden to the Council of the Royal Society dated Piccadilly 13 May 1790.

23 cm

Photocopy of the manuscript in the Royal Society MM.3.30

Outraged at the slurs cast on his 'professional character', and in so 'respectable a place as at a meeting of the Royal Society', Ramsden composed a detailed vindication of his actions in a letter to the Council of the Royal Society dated 5 May 1790.

'Nothing could equal my surprize', he declares, 'on hearing the charges brought against me . . . by Major General Roy'. He continues 'I was the more affected by it as coming from a Gentleman with whom I considered myself in Friendship'. Distressed that the defamatory manuscript had already been shown to King George III, Ramsden was anxious to present a 'true statement of the facts alluded to in the Generals paper', and no doubt felt the more aggrieved since he had spent considerable time in constructing the various instruments 'to the neglect of a more lucrative business and chiefly with a view to the advancement of Science and the honour of this Country'. His detailed explanations of his conduct finally secured the erasure of the more provocative passages from Roy's paper.

77 The Expurgated Account

'An account of the Trigonometrical Operation, whereby the Distance between the Meridians of the Royal Observatories of Greenwich and Paris has been determined'. By Major-General William Roy F.R.S. and A.S. *Philosophical Transactions*, Vol. LXXX, pt. I, 1790.

25 cm

BL Department of Printed Books L.R.292

Published posthumously, this account contained few of the original references to the acrimonious dispute with Ramsden. Page 127 of the *Philosophical Transactions*, when compared with the corresponding text of the manuscript draft, provides an example of the omissions of the printed paper.

A monumental narrative of a geodetic operation which was 'the first of its kind in this country', the paper comprises eight sections describing the instruments and techniques employed and the results of the trigonometrical observations. It concludes with a persuasive argument in favour of continuing the triangulation 'over the whole island' to form the basis of a national survey.

78 Jesse Ramsden (1753–1800)

Illustration on facing page

I. Ramsden, Optician to His Majesty. Painted by R. Home. Engraved by John Jones. London, Pub^{d} . . . Jany the 1st. 1791 by Messrs. Molteno Colnaghi and Co., Pall Mall.

66 × 51 cm

BM Department of Prints and Drawings 1841-11-13-17

Born in Halifax in 1735, Ramsden became an apprentice to Burton, a mathematical instrument maker, in London in 1758. Here he mastered the skill of engraving and set up independently in business in 1762. He married the daughter of John Dollond, the optician, in 1765. The ingenious inventor of machines for engraving accurate divisions on mathematical instruments, and the first to use the vernier on circular instruments, Ramsden also built in 1789 the famous five-foot vertical circle shown in this portrait. Designed to replace quadrants and sextants, it was used in the Palermo Observatory.

Ramsden reached the height of his profession with the construction of the three-foot theodolite in 1787. His obsession with perfection resulted in prolonged delays in the delivery of most of his instruments, and led to the dispute with Roy. His total disregard for time is illustrated by the occasion on which 'he attended at Buckingham House precisely, he supposed at the time named in the royal mandate'. The King remarked that he was 'punctual as to the day and hour, while late by a whole year'.

79 The Great Theodolite

Illustration overleaf

General View of the Instrument. From *Account of the . . . Trigonometrical Survey of England and Wales.* By William Mudge and Isaac Dalby. Vol. I, London, W. Faden, 1799.

33 × 18 cm

BL Map Library Maps Ref. G.2b

Known as the 'father of accurate theodolites', this 'Great Circular Instrument' was ordered by Roy from Jesse Ramsden in 1784. Use of the new theodolite was essential to achieve the highest degree of accuracy in angular and linear measurements; and Roy could not proceed with the triangulation of south-east England without it. Two years later, in 1786, he was still waiting for the instrument to be completed. Now a man of sixty and in poor health, he complained: 'it is hard upon me to have this operation hanging over my head for another year, without any fault of mine: But with such a man as Ramsden there is no help for it'.

Three feet in diameter and weighing over 200 lb, the theodolite was the first instrument capable of reading a mark at 70 miles' distance with an angular error of only two seconds. The instrument was transported in a sprung van and for some observations had to be elevated to a height of

thirty feet on a specially constructed scaffold. The theodolite was finally delivered to Roy in July 1787, and after his death in 1790 was in use by the Ordnance Survey from 1799 until 1853. Stored in the Survey's Office at Southampton, it was destroyed by enemy action in the Second World War.

80 Ramsden's Second 3ft Theodolite

Photograph of the original instrument

By courtesy of the Science Museum London

Known as the '3-ft. O.S.', this second 'great theodolite', made by Ramsden in 1791, was apparently intended for use by the East India Company. The Duke of Richmond, Master General of the Ordnance, arranged for the purchase of this improved instrument which was used on the Trigonometrical Survey for some years from 1791.

81 The French Connection

Plan of the Triangles connecting the Meridians of the Royal Observatories of Greenwich and Paris. From *An Account of the . . . Trigonometrical Survey of England and Wales*. By William Mudge and Isaac Dalby. London, W. Faden, 1799.

33 × 65 cm

BL Map Library Maps Ref. G.2b

A fine example of international geodetic co-operation, the triangulation of south-east England was proposed by Cassini de Thury (1714–84), Director of the Paris Observatory, as a method of resolving the disagreement between English and French astronomers regarding the difference in longitude between the Greenwich and Paris Observatories. Under the direction of the Royal Society, Roy was to undertake the triangulation from the vicinity of Greenwich to the coast near Dover; there, by means of cross-channel observations, to link up with the French triangulations already completed near Calais.

The measurements for this, the final scientific survey of Roy's career, occupied most of the remaining six years of his life. With the long awaited delivery of Ramsden's theodolite in July 1787, the operations continued until they were completed in 1789.

The cross-channel measurements, finished in October 1787, were 'to establish for ever the triangular connection between the two countries'. While it did not settle the immediate dispute, Roy's work had a profound effect on the future of British map-making, leading to the continuation of the work by the Board of Ordnance in 1791 to become what is known today as the Ordnance Survey.

82 Roy's Expenses on the Triangulation

Major Gen[l] Roy's Account of the Expenditure of £2,000 received by him from Sir Joseph Banks . . . for carrying on the Trigonometrical Operation.

32 cm

Photocopy of the manuscript in the Royal Society D.M.4-23

This account of Roy's expenditure of £2,000 between 1784 and 1788 shows his meticulous preparations for the triangulation which began in 1787. Scaffolds were constructed by 'Saunders the Carpenter' to mount the theodolite at various points, lamps were purchased from 'Smith the

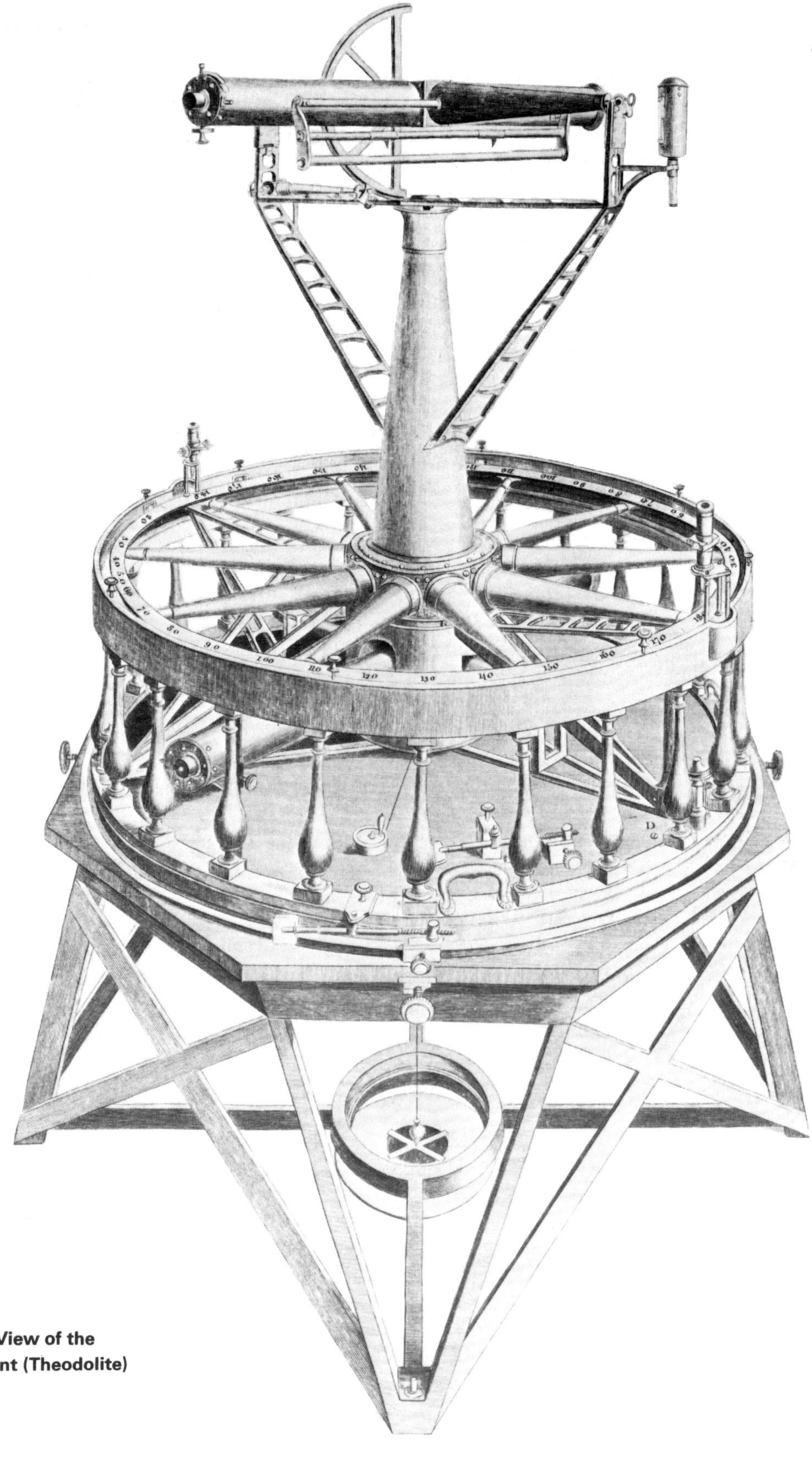

79 General View of the Instrument (Theodolite)

Tinman' to illuminate the brass circle of the theodolite in night observations, and experiments were made with white lights. Consisting of '28 parts of Nitre, 4 parts of Sulphur and two parts of orpiment [trisulphate of arsenic] powdered fine' the lights were designed to be burnt in copper cups set on a tripod. It was by this means that the 'most distant stations could be rendered visible'.

83 The Honour of the Nation

Lisbon, Seen from the Quinta da Torrinha Val de Pereiro. Drawn by L. B. Parkyns. Engraved by W. J. Bennett. [*c.* 1810.]

33 × 50 cm

BL Map Library K.Top. LXXIV.66-c.3

In constant poor health, and suffering from a lung complaint, Roy travelled to Lisbon in November 1789 to recuperate. His visit lasted six months and he returned to London in April 1790. He died suddenly at his home in Argyll Street on 1 July, without having corrected the last pages of the proofs of his paper for the Royal Society. In the conclusion to the paper he had written that:

> 'The Writer of this Account cannot help considering it as being incumbent on him to recommend, that the trigonometrical operation, so successfully begun, should certainly be continued, and gradually extended over the whole Island. Compared with the greatness of the object, the annual expense to the public would be a mere trifle . . . The honour of the nation is concerned in having at least as good a map of this as there is of any other country'.

That it was accomplished by others was truly his epitaph.

84 Roy's Last Home

Photograph of No. 10 Argyll Street, London W.1

Roy moved from his residence at 32–35 Great Pulteney Street, where he had lived since 1765, to 12 Argyll Street in 1779. Here he died 'after two hours illness' in the early hours of Thursday morning, 1 July 1790. He is reported to have been 'on business at the War Office till eight o'clock on Wednesday night'. Roy was buried in the Parish of St James, Westminster, on 7 July. No record remains of his burial at St James Church, Piccadilly, and he was probably interred in the parish burial ground, Hampstead Road, N.W.1, which was converted into a public garden in 1887.

The formation of Argyll Place in 1820, which followed on the construction of Regent Street, led to the re-numbering of the houses in Argyll Street. Roy's house, No. 12, became No. 10, and, although much altered, is one of only two original Argyll estate buildings to survive.

85 General Sir David Dundas 1735–1820

Illustration on facing page

General, The Rt Honble Sir David Dundas, K.B. Engrav'd for the Royal Military Panorama. by H. R. Cook, from a Picture by W. Owen, R.A. *c.*1802

29 × 30 cm

BM Department of Prints and Drawings 1866-11-10-1329

Born in Edinburgh in 1735, Dundas was educated at the Royal Military Academy Woolwich and joined the Survey of Scotland under Roy when he was about seventeen years old. Roy and Dundas evidently formed an immediate friendship which continued through the following years of

85 General Sir David Dundas

reconnoitring in the south of England with Dundas's uncle, David Watson. After the end of the war with France in 1763, Dundas began his long study of tactics, writing the *Principles of Military Movements*. Published in 1788, the book established Dundas as the foremost tactician of the century. Having achieved the rank of Major General in 1790, he went on to become Quartermaster General at the Horse Guards in 1796, and was promoted General in 1802. 'A tall, spare man, crabbed and austere, dry in his demeanour', Dundas was appointed executor of Roy's will, which was dated 13 November 1786. Roy bequeathed all his 'Manuscripts Orderly Books and Drawings relative to Prince Ferdinand's campaigns in Germany' to Dundas who he thought was 'well qualified to extract something useful from rough materials of that sort'.

Select Reading List

CHALMERS, George. *Caledonia.* London, 1810.

CLOSE, Sir Charles. *The early years of the Ordnance Survey.* A reprint with a new introduction by J. B. Harley. Newton Abbot, 1969.

HARLEY, J. B. and O'DONOGHUE, Y. *The Old Series Ordnance Survey Maps of England and Wales.* Vol. I. Lympne Castle, Kent, 1975.

MACDONALD, George. 'General William Roy and his Military Antiquities of the Romans in North Britain'. *Archaeologia*, second series, Vol. XVIII. London, 1917.

ROY, William. 'An Account of the Mode proposed to be followed in determining the relative Situation of the Royal Observatories of Greenwich and Paris'. Royal Society, *Philosophical Transactions*, Vol. LXXVII. London, 1787.

SKELTON, R. A. *The Military Survey of Scotland.* The Royal Scottish Geographical Society, Special Publication no. 1. Edinburgh, 1967.

SKELTON, R. A. 'The origins of the Ordnance Survey of Great Britain'. *Geographical Journal*, Vol. CXXVIII. London, 1962.